Lifting the Lid
An Ecological Approach to Toilet Systems

Peter Harper & Louise Halestrap

CENTRE FOR
ALTERNATIVE
TECHNOLOGY
PUBLICATIONS

© C.A.T. Publications August 1999

The Centre for Alternative Technology Machynlleth, Powys, SY20 9AZ, UK

Tel. 01654 702400 • **Fax.** 01654 702782

E-mail: help@catinfo.demon.co.uk • **Web page:** www.cat.org.uk

Assistance

Illustrations Maritsa Kelly, Roger Kelly, Graham Preston and John Urry

Cover Photographs Peter Harper

Edited by Stokely Webster

ISBN 1 898049 79 3

3 4 5 6 7 8 9

Mail Order copies from: Buy Green By Mail   Tel. 01654 703409

The details are provided in good faith and believed to be correct at the time of writing, however no responsibility is taken for any errors. Our publications are updated regularly; please let us know of any amendments or additions which you think may be useful for future editions.

Printed in Great Britain by Biddles Ltd. (01483 502224) on chlorine free paper obtained from sustainable sources.

Foreword

The conventional flush toilet is an environmental disaster. It could scarcely be better designed to waste one of the world's most overstretched resources: fresh water. Every time we pull the chain, the future of the world is sucked a little further down the drain.

Part of the problem is that the flush toilet has been introduced, like so many labour-saving devices, as a universal solution to a multiplicity of problems. It is deployed all over the world, whether or not local water supplies or sewage treatment facilities are adequate. The water closet has become the symbol of civilisation.

Lifting the Lid flushes away our preconceptions about the toilet. It shows that the massive task of disposing of or treating human waste in different circumstances can be tackled by a host of different means, which don't compromise the survival of future generations. It ventures further into the mechanics of the lavatory than most of us have ever cared to go before, and the solutions it discovers are innovative and extraordinary. This is, I can confidently assert, the best toilet paper you're ever likely to read.

George Monbiot, August 1999

Acknowledgements

We gratefully acknowledge the enormous contributions made to this book by Andy Warren, Nick Grant and Mark Moodie, Britain's poineers of dry toilet design.

Other colleagues (or ex-colleagues) we would like to thank include Chris Weedon, Stokely Webster, Marcus Zipperlen, Maritsa Kelly, Roger Kelly, Jeremy Light and Clive Newman. We would also like the thank the following individuals or organisations for their kind cooperation:

Aquatron (Sweden)
Bee Environmental Ltd
Biolet
Tom and Lisa Brown
Leigh Davison
De Twaalf Ambachten
DOWMUS
Ekolet
Ekologen (Sweden)
Globemall
Jeremy Harris and Claire Adamson
Hepworths Ltd
Joe Jenkins

Kingsley Clivus Ltd
Sietz Leeflang
George Monbiot
Tara Oy (Finland)
Jack Parsons
Peak District National Park
Septum (Sweden)
Servator
South Somerset District Council
Tal-y-llyn Railway
Thetford Services
Waterless UK Ltd
Wendage

Contents

Absurdly, the hardest part of producing this book was thinking of a title. Authors and publishers have different axes to grind, and personal taste varies more in this field than any other. The *New Futures* series aims at an enthusiastic lay audience and prefers witty, allusive titles to ponderous self-explanation such as, *An Introduction to Water-Saving Toilet Systems*. But, of course, in this field any play on words is likely to appear facetious or to stray across the boundary of acceptable taste – if we can even agree where that boundary lies. So, inevitably, there was much cudgelling of brains to find the perfect title that would please everyone. *Lifting the Lid* is a compromise title, but on the way to it so many clever solutions emerged that we felt it would be a shame not to share some of the rejected candidates with our readers.

Raising the Bog Standard
Busted Flush
Green Grow the Flushes O
Low Water Loos
Looping the Loo
Against the Flow
After the Deluge
Noye's Flusshe
Ye Gods and Little Flushes!
Out of the (Water) Closet
Lore of Ordure
Dung Roamin
Peepoo!
Dropping Hints
New Lavs for Old
Just the Job
Green and Pleasant Lavs

Loos: The Plot
Patience on a Pedestal
Flush Finish
Sitting Bull
Beyond the Pail
S*itting Pretty
The Bottom Line
On Where You Sit
Nothing to Loos
Re: Sitting
The Crystal Bowl
Where e'er you Sit
Are You S*itting Comfortably
Doing the Job
Taking the Piss and Winning the Poo
The Way to Little Flushing

Introduction

This is a book about alternatives to the ordinary flush toilet, otherwise known as the water closet or WC. It is not a crusade against the WC. From a user's point of view the WC works extremely well, and any attempt to replace it on a mass scale would surely lead to riots in the streets! But the 'bog standard' WC is not always the best choice. Reasons for looking at alternatives come from three main directions:

- **Practical** – of particular interest to rural householders with no sewer connection, or to organisations responsible for public toilets in remote sites
- **Political or economic** – driven by the rapid growth of demand for water and especially relevant to water companies, government agencies, businesses and property developers
- **Environmental** – generally voiced by 'green' activists, forward-looking architects and designers and those concerned, either personally or professionally, with sustainability.

Is it for you? Responses to an earlier version (called *Fertile Waste: Managing your Domestic Sewage*) and enquiries to the CAT information service, suggest the following categories of readers for whom this could be a useful book:

- Owners of existing properties without any sanitation facilities at all
- Self-builders wishing to know the full range of possibilities before making a choice
- Householders with a septic tank system which is not working, or is failing to meet Environmental Agency discharge standards
- Householders wanting to have a second toilet facility in the garden or grounds without necessarily providing a water supply or drains

- Householders with an installed commercial dry-toilet system wanting to know about the principles behind it
- Boat-owners wanting to explore compact alternatives for ship-board toilets
- Architects wishing to specify alternative systems, in particular waterless toilets, or to redesign a building to accommodate one
- Planning and public health officials wanting to know whether to grant permission for a proposed installation
- Policymakers wishing to know the full range of technical possibilities
- Water companies exploring options in minimising water demand or sewage volumes
- Developers wanting to maximise sustainability and environmental quality of a new development
- Parks officials or leisure developers wondering how to provide public toilet facilities in remote areas
- Academics teaching courses in environmental topics, and their students
- Development workers concerned with sanitation in developing countries
- Professionals in environmental engineering wishing to catch up with progress at the small end of things
- Green householders concerned to reduce their personal impact on the environment
- Environmental activists wishing to promote awareness of radical solutions
- Eco-enthusiasts keen to pioneer and evaluate new practical approaches.

This is a wide range of different agendas, but we shall try to bear you all in mind!

THE STRUCTURE OF THE BOOK

Even for those who worship other sanitary gods, the WC remains a powerful totem that demands tribute. Accordingly, Chapter One pays due homage to the WC, then lists its drawbacks. Chapter Two makes it clear that the thing you sit on is usually part of a larger TOILET SYSTEM, then describes the most common toilet systems to put the contents of this book in a wider context. Two major types of system emerge from this review: the 'wet', where the WC is retained in some form, and the 'dry' where water usage is reduced to an absolute minimum. This book deliberately focuses on dry systems and Chapter Three describes the principles on which they work. Chapter Four shows how the principles are applied in practice, with particular attention to 'composting toilets'. Chapter Five is a gallery of case studies, warts and all. There is no shortage of warts in this field.

While dry systems are laudable, dirty water of various kinds still needs to be dealt with. To provide a comprehensive one-stop shop we include a 'wet' section dealing with Water Usage (Chapter Six), Septic Tanks (Chapter Seven) and Greywater (Chapter Eight). These chapters will all be useful to householders or organisations wishing to improve their toilet systems without necessarily abandoning flush toilets or investing in costly 'alternative' sewage installations. Chapter Nine looks at the nutrient/fertiliser aspect of toilet systems and suggests ways in which they could be integrated into the other nutrient flows in a house-and-garden.

Finally in the Appendices we give specific instructions for two DIY waterless toilets, a glossary and an index. Terms defined in the glossary are written in SMALL CAPITALS when they first appear. Notes and references are indicated by superscript numbers (e.g. [1]) and listed at the end of the book.

THE RELIABILITY OF INFORMATION IN THIS BOOK

The development of the various systems described here has been going on for many years, but there is much that we do not fully understand. There is no definitive theory or comprehensive body of experience that can guarantee success. Many of these systems are biological and work only within certain limits. There is an irreducible element of creative chaos in biology, and sometimes a complex biological system will go off in a completely unexpected direction. It is impossible to give rules which will always work under any circumstances. On the other hand biological toilet systems are flexible and intelligent, and a dialogue develops in which both toilet system and user learn to operate with the other's quirks and preferences. Things improve with time and experience.

A reported success therefore, is not necessarily one which can be mechanically reproduced. Nor is a reported failure to be taken as the *coup de grâce*. We are still learning, and it is important not to take anything in this book as the last word.

COMPLEMENTARY PUBLICATIONS
As published, the book lacks an important element, the *Sewage Treatment Resource Guide*, an up-to-date listing of publications, organisations and manufacturers available separately from CAT[1]. Printed in the book this would quickly get out of date, so it is produced separately and updated yearly.

Lifting the Lid is complementary to another in this New Futures series, *Sewage Solutions: Answering the Call of Nature*[2]. While there is a certain amount of deliberate overlap, the real enthusiast should probably have both. *Sewage Solutions* is the 'wet' book, dealing with sewage liquids; this is the 'dry' book, dealing with sewage solids, and how to avoid or at least minimise the generation of foul liquids.

Other books which overlap with this one, or on which we have drawn heavily, are *Septic Tanks: An Overview* by Nick Grant and Mark Moodie, *Create an Oasis with Greywater* by Art Ludwig, and *Safe to Drink?* by Julie Stauffer[3].

A NOTE ON TERMINOLOGY AND STYLE
An unavoidable difficulty in a book of this kind is the balance between sober gentility and calling a spade a spade. It is not an academic textbook. It aims to be practical and accessible, and the constant use of polite euphemisms can get a bit tiresome. At the same time the book is likely to be used in (for example) planning circles to inform and persuade councillors or senior colleagues that

certain alternatives are worth considering, so a certain element of decorum is required. On this account, we have not adopted the hilarious frankness of *The Humanure Handbook* or *Das Scheiss Buch*[4]. Although pretty well everybody calls it shit in private we are going to use more cumbersome but respectable terms such as faeces, faecal matter, sewage solids, toilet wastes etc. Sorry!

Chapter One
The Mighty WC

There is a famous passage in *The Communist Manifesto* where Marx and Engels generously acknowledge the qualities and achievements of capitalism. You may want to change it, they argue, but do not underestimate its awesome powers, both functional and cultural. A century and a half later capitalism has indeed swept all before it. Those who haven't got it want it, and those that have cannot imagine anything else.

In the sanitary sphere it is much the same with the mighty WC. It is so overwhelmingly dominant that the alternatives have become almost unthinkable. Its qualities are not only practical but richly symbolic. In developing societies it is the principal badge of progress and modernity, while in already-modern societies it is one of the non-negotiable pillars of ordinary life – ranking above the car, the central heating and the holiday abroad. The WC is not just an appliance, it is an icon.

Since the WC inevitably sets the standards for any other kind of toilet system, let us (in the spirit of Marx and Engels) catalogue its virtues:

FOR THE WC
> • **It is hygienic**
> This is because:
> the water in the bowl forms an effective seal between the toilet and the drain
> the glazed surface is easy to keep clean
> PATHOGENIC material is quickly removed

- **It *feels* hygienic**

This is probably even more important. It is said that in the very early days of the WC people found it strange and offensive, but without doubt it has now become a touchstone of modern respectability.

- **Flushing is symbolically satisfying**

The process of flushing has become a ritual act of purification and 'completed business'. It provides a gratifying sense of removing corruption to a remote place, out of sight/out of mind.

- **It is familiar and does not provoke anxiety**

There is always a residue of unease associated with toilets. For this reason householders are grateful for something which is so familiar it fades into the background and does not excite notice or comment.

- **It is easy to operate and everybody knows how to use it**

This is especially advantageous with guests, and helps both them and their hosts to feel at ease about sanitary arrangements. No instructions or additional thought are required.

- **It requires minimum maintenance**

Just regular cleaning, which again everybody knows how to do, and very occasional attention to flushing mechanisms.

- **It is reliable and very rarely misfunctions**

Even embarrassing accidents involving small children are quickly cleaned up. Blocked drains and breakdowns of the flush mechanism are the commonest faults, usually rectified with little fuss.

- **It makes no attempt to treat the material put into it**

Since this part of the operation is not the user's responsibility everything is simplified, and householders cannot make mistakes that have serious consequences.

- **It is very compact**

The fact that the WC is merely a collection device means that it will fit into almost any bathroom situation. Many alternative systems are too large for this.

- **The requirement for water is compatible with the need for some system to deal with other waste waters from the building.**

Almost any serviced building produces waste water other than foul water, and this has to be dealt with in any case. The WC then shares the basic infrastructure costs of sewerage with greywater and storm drains.

• **Water is an effective way of transporting solid material horizontally**

Material can be removed efficiently and automatically to a convenient treatment site even if there is no sewer connection.

• **There is no direct energy requirement**

Occasionally pumps are required both for supply or drainage, but a WC flush typically operates from mains pressure and drains by gravity. Energy is used in sewage treatment plants and for sludge disposal, but less *pro rata* than some alternative systems.

This is a formidable list, and a hard act to follow. Why might we want to consider alternatives?

AGAINST THE WC

• **It consumes a large quantity of fresh drinking water**

The consumption of water has a definite environmental impact. Toilet flushing is the largest single use of water in households and, at least for metered consumers, it costs money.

• **It pollutes water**

Dirty water has to be cleaned, and this also has an environmental impact. If it is *not* cleaned it has an even larger environmental impact.

• **It leads to the generation of sewage sludge**

The generation of sewage sludge at 20 million tonnes a year in the UK is as much as all other household refuse. Most sludge is contaminated with heavy metals, largely from domestic sources, entering via the sewer system. It is a continuing environmental problem.

• **It combines solid and liquid**

Treating sewage solids or sewage liquids separately is relatively easy; it is far harder when they are mixed, especially when diluted with large quantities of fresh water. Dilution also makes the recovery of nutrients harder.

• **It is dependent on a reliable water supply and drainage**

A WC cannot operate where there is no water supply or where there is no possibility of a drain. Even where water and drainage can be provided, this is sometimes awkward and can clutter up a small bathroom with inconvenient and unsightly pipework.

* **It is not *perfectly* hygienic**

Ordinary flushing can generate splashes and BIO-AEROSOLS containing human pathogens, all avoided by dry toilets.

* **There *are* some drawbacks of gentility**

Splashing during use can be unpleasant and there are usually odours, if only temporary. Some alternative systems have overcome these problems. Flushing and urinating noises can make going to the toilet a semi-public act. This is not the case with dry systems.

* **It is open to serious abuse**

The existence of a direct and anonymous connection to the sewer can tempt householders to dispose of materials that can contaminate millions of litres of water or recovered sludge.

* **It offends some ethical sensibilities**

Some people find it positively offensive to contaminate drinking water with pathogenic waste, and value the opportunity to take responsibility for their own wastes.

* **It conflicts with long-term sustainability**

In the long run sustainability requires the closing of many loops in the flow of materials, including food, biological wastes and plant nutrients. Conventional sanitation makes this more difficult.

ARE 'ALTERNATIVE' TOILETS ALWAYS THE GREENEST SOLUTION?

Often, but not necessarily. In designing or specifying alternatives we have to be very clear about what we are actually trying to achieve, and whether in any given case 'alternative sanitation systems' are the best way of achieving them. The environmental movement is not immune from its own kind of consumerism, and many would-be green householders suppose that merely possessing items like solar panels, double glazing and a can-crusher renders them instantly sustainable. A dry toilet can be just the same, a green fashion accessory which makes very little difference to the wider environment, or may even make things worse.

Looking at it from an individual point of view, it is important to consider the whole picture of your life (or your operation, if you are an institution) to ensure that resources are being used effectively. There is no point in large sacrifices of money, time or convenience for a relatively small return if more effective ways of achieving the same result are available. For example, if your principal aim were to generate on-site fertility for crops, composting faeces might seem obvious and logical; yet a higher yield of nutrients can be obtained from composting kitchen and garden waste, and/or using urine, with much simpler and safer processes (see Chapter Nine for more details on nutrient cycling). Another example: if one of your aims were water conservation it would not make much sense to have a dry toilet *and* a swimming pool.

By installing a system for your own use, you may achieve important environmental goals such as reducing personal water consumption and pollution. Yet from a wider perspective, we have to acknowledge that TAKE-UP of environmentally sound solutions will be much greater if they fit easily into the patterns and tastes of modern life. So, from a general environmental point of view it might be more rational to promote the most *acceptable* rather than the most *efficient* systems. Some simple arithmetic makes the point: if toilet flushing takes typically 35% of household water consumption, a totally waterless toilet could save this much per household. But if it were adopted by only 1% of households the overall effect on water consumption would be a mere 0.35%. In contrast, low flush WCs saving 'only' 20% of household water but adopted by 50% of households would give an overall saving of 10% – thirty times more.

THE PSYCHOLOGY OF TOILETS
It is important to recognise that psychological factors dominate anything associated with toilets. Excrement is not only physically but *culturally* contaminating[1], and needs to be kept apart from other aspects of daily life not just physically, but mentally as well. In ordinary polite society there is felt to be a necessary hypocrisy which pretends that bowel functions don't really happen. We don't

want to be reminded of them, or of what they produce. Quite apart from its wonderful capacity to make ORDURE vanish in the twinkling of an eye, the cleanliness and ordinariness of the WC helps it to fade into the background, easily edited out of consciousness. Even slight differences can disturb this delicate social theatre and stir up uncomfortable feelings. None of us can escape this entirely.

At the same time there are contradictory elements in which revulsion and anxiety are mixed with fascination and, of course, humour. Such feelings are extremely complex, ambivalent and subjective, as William Ian Miller illustrates in his brilliant study *The Anatomy of Disgust*.[2] They are not necessarily fixed, and what is repulsive in one context can become ordinary or even attractive in another. The implication is that the take-up of novel and alternative toilet systems in mass society is likely to be determined by fickle dynamics of private and public taste and have little to do with their objective merits. This cuts both ways. It could work against the adoption of alternatives, but equally, in the right circumstances, could see resistance crumble and even go into reverse.

However, for the time being we can say that the WC in some form will be a reference point, setting a standard of convenience, hygiene, gentility, and reassuring normality by which any other toilet system must be judged. We shall refer to this as the PORCELAIN STANDARD.

Chapter Two
Toilet Systems

This short chapter presents an overview of the sanitation systems likely to be encountered in the UK. It shows the main differences between 'conventional' and 'alternative' approaches, and where they overlap.

Humans do not excrete at random. Even in the most 'primitive' societies there are particular places where defecation takes place, usually at a distance from dwellings and social activities. Raw faeces are not only unpleasant but dangerous. They must be kept separate until they are made safe by some kind of *treatment* process, natural or otherwise.

Treatment is the critical element. What we colloquially call a 'toilet' – the thing you sit on or wee into – does not usually *treat* human wastes. It simply collects them for treatment elsewhere. For clarity we shall call this the TOILET PEDESTAL. The pedestal is only one part of what we shall call a TOILET SYSTEM. A toilet system includes *collection, treatment,* and where necessary, *transport* between the two. There is a limited number of possible ways to do each of these three things, and some combinations don't work. Practical toilet systems therefore fall into just a few main types. For those planning new sanitary arrangements or modifications of existing ones it is useful to be aware of standard examples and to see which 'alternatives' can be applied in each part of a system. You will also need to be aware of the legal and planning implications of your choices (see Box 2.1).

In most conventional toilet systems material is transported by flowing water. The water and its suspended contents run through a SEWER connection to a remote treatment plant. If there is no sewer connection the water must either be stored pending collection by tanker, or treated on-site. If water is *not* used solid material must be regularly removed for treatment elsewhere, or must be treated on the spot in close proximity to the pedestal. The main possibilities are summarised in figure 2.1, although these diagrams ignore the question of GREYWATER, dealt with in Chapter Eight, and the special case of URINALS (Chapter Six).

Fig. 2.1

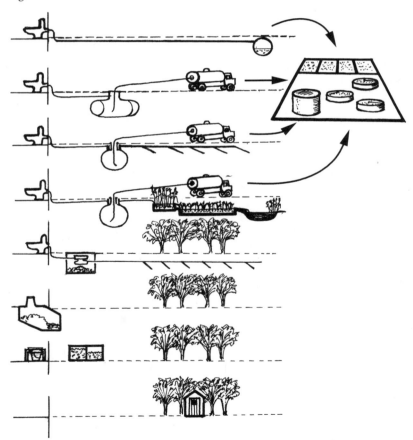

Fig. 2.1 Classification of toilet systems. Schematic layout of eight representative systems – explanations overleaf.

A CLASSIFICATION OF TOILET SYSTEMS

I: With WC

a: With sewer connection
Standard WC or Urinal ⟶ sewer ⟶ sewage works

Solids and liquids to sewage works

This applies to 96% of toilets in the UK. The only variation under the control of a householder is in the particular type of WC or urinal used, which includes
- Building regulations standard: less than 7.5 litres flush
- Proposed building regulations standard: less than 6 litres flush
- Dual flush
- State-of-the-art low-flush: 2-4 litres
- Urine-separating
- Vacuum
- Foam
- Controlled-flush and waterless urinals

These variants (not mutually exclusive) can apply in most situations where a standard WC is used. They can make a great deal of difference to overall water consumption. They are discussed further in Chapter Five. Having a mains connection does not preclude other alternatives but changes the rationale for installing them.

b: With no Sewer Connection
1: On-site collection but no treatment
WC ⟶ collection tank or cesspool ⟶ sewage works

Solids and liquids
transported to sewage works

Temporary toilets for public events usually have no sewer connection. The WC flushes with an antiseptic fluid and runs into a collection tank which is eventually emptied by tanker. In some rural areas a house toilet is served by the same system. The tank is sometimes called a CESSPOOL. A cesspool is not the same as a SEPTIC TANK, and merely serves to hold all the sewage until it needs emptying, which is usually every few weeks. This is expensive and inefficient and virtually any of the systems discussed in this book would be an improvement.

2: On-site treatment of liquid effluent
WC or urinal ⟶ septic tank ⟶ leachfield

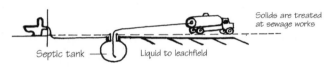

This currently applies to over 90% of on-site treatment systems. In fact only the liquids are treated on-site, while most of the solids are removed from time to time for conventional off-site treatment. Septic tanks and LEACHFIELDS are discussed in more detail in Chapter Six.

WC ⟶ septic tank ⟶ various alternatives to the treatment of liquid effluents

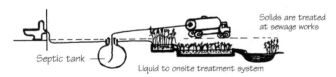

This includes such techniques as filter beds, aeration plants, reedbeds and treatment ponds. Once again the solids are usually treated off-site, although in the right circumstances on-site systems are possible. These are beyond the scope of this book, and are covered by *Sewage Solutions*.

WC plus rapid physical separation of solids for on-site treatment

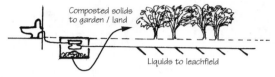

This is a relatively new and little-known category. After the WC (or variants) the solids and liquids are separated, either by filtration or surface-tension effects, before the solids have a chance to break up and disperse in the liquid. The solids can then be treated by composting processes and the liquids by any of the above methods. This approach has the advantage of retaining the WC and being able to use water (temporarily) to transport material at least some distance from the toilet pedestal, and it replaces the septic tank. It offers the possibility of complete on-site treatment, and is discussed further in Chapter Four, with a case study in Chapter Five.

II: Without WC

a: Toilets with *in situ* treatment

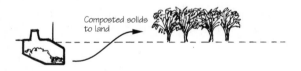

Here, treatment takes place within or close to the pedestal
1. Composting toilets Treatment is by biological decomposition
2. De-watering toilets Treatment is by dehydration and pasteurisation
3. Incinerating toilets Treatment is by total combustion

b: Bucket Toilets

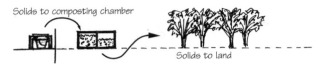

Solids to composting chamber

Solids to land

Treatment takes place remotely from the pedestal

1. Liquid chemical toilets Using a sterilising fluid

2. Dry bucket toilets Using a dry SOAK material or nothing at all

c: Privies

Privies are a special historical case, and where still in use may

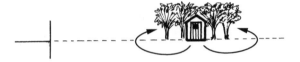

combine elements of the other types

Other unusual toilet systems are found outside the UK, with generous variety in the tropics.[1] This book will focus on types applicable in Europe, with particular emphasis on low-water or no-water systems, to which the next two chapters are dedicated.

Box 2.1

The Legal and Planning Aspects of Unconventional Toilet Systems:

Public health is important, and public authorities are right to be concerned about toilet systems. It's part of their job. Generally if you are planning anything unusual you should let them know, and indeed, seek their advice. The relevant agencies – the Planning Dept of the Local Authority, the Building Regulations Officer, the Environmental Health Officer and the Environment Agency (or SEPA in Scotland) might or might not be familiar with what you are proposing, but it is best to explain everything as fully and openly as you can. Usually they are sympathetic and helpful. They cannot stop you using an unusual system if it does not cause a nuisance, threaten public health or damage the environment, but in some cases they can insist that a conventional system be installed, even if you choose not to use it! If you encounter difficulties, try giving them a copy of this book.

Chapter Three
The Biology of Breakdown

In this chapter we look in more detail at toilet systems which do not include a WC, and which treat the material on-site. Since the processes are mostly biological we start with a summary of the basic biology of composting which will help to make sense of everything else. Then we discuss the main factors which influence the efficiency of the process, and how they relate to the design of dry toilets.

THE BIOLOGY OF BREAKDOWN

The biochemistry of life can get complicated, but behind it is a simple principle of complexity-from-simplicity and back again. It is a kind of biological Lego™ based on two very basic materials: carbon dioxide and water.

Fig. 3.1

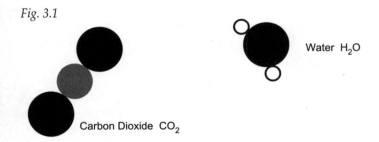

Water H_2O

Carbon Dioxide CO_2

95% of living matter is made up from these two very simple compounds. The black circles are oxygen atoms.

Fig. 3.1 Biological Lego™.

Plants build up complex organic matter from these two substances plus a small quantity of minerals dissolved in the water. Oxygen is left as a by-product. The process is elegantly counter-balanced by its mirror image, which takes place in nearly all organisms. Combining organic matter with oxygen releases energy and regenerates the original raw material – carbon dioxide, water and minerals (Figure 3.2). On a world scale the two processes control each other, so all the different components remain at about the same level. This helps to regulate the composition of the atmosphere and the global climate.

Fig. 3.2

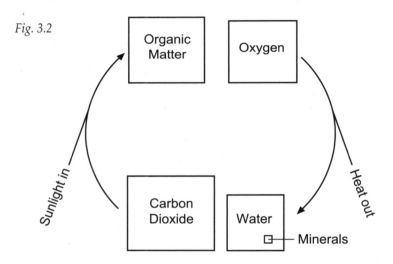

The size of the boxes is roughly proportional to the weights of the components.

Fig. 3.2 The basic carbon/energy cycle in nature.

In nature most DECOMPOSITION processes involve the descending limb of this cycle, and that is what we are aiming at in our biological toilets. In theory organic matter should turn completely into CO_2 and water, and disperse back into the biosphere. In practice other things can happen on the way. For example some of the organic matter and minerals can turn into forms which break down much more slowly, and tend to accumulate as complex, stable, dark-coloured materials like coal, peat and HUMUS. These have significant roles to play in the biosphere: humus is particularly important acting as a store of energy and minerals for soil organisms, promoting the formation of soils and maintaining soil structure. Compost is home-made humus. What we are trying to achieve in both compost heaps and biological toilets is HUMIFICATION, a process that turns much of the organic matter into carbon dioxide and water, but leaves a residue of odourless, hygienic and useful soil-like material.

The breakdown process is driven by a wide range of DECOMPOSER ORGANISMS. The following factors all make a difference to the rate at which breakdown proceeds, mostly because of their effect on the decomposers:

- Oxygen
- Temperature
- Moisture levels
- Carbon to Nitrogen ratio
- Availability of nutrients and carbon
- Special organisms
- Toxic materials.

Theoretically, optimising all these factors in a compost toilet would lead to very rapid rates of breakdown and require only a small, cheap chamber which could be fitted into a tight space. But in practice they sometimes conflict with each other, and getting things absolutely right costs money, time or effort and may not be worth it if speed is not a problem. We should look for reasonable, practical compromises. Let us look at these factors in more detail.

THE DIMENSIONS OF BREAKDOWN
Oxygen
Ideally, your composting process generates carbon dioxide, water and humus, all of which are harmless and do not smell. The process also releases heat which stimulates the decomposers and keeps the whole thing moving along. These ideal conditions are called AEROBIC.

Logically you cannot make two substances that are made of mostly oxygen without oxygen to begin with (see Figure 3.1). If there is not enough oxygen the decomposition process cannot turn everything fully into carbon dioxide and water. Instead, compounds with less oxygen are produced, and these tend to be smelly or poisonous and do not generate heat. Conditions with too little oxygen are called ANAEROBIC, and we would like to avoid them in our toilets. Unfortunately toilet wastes have a consistency that can easily form a dense, soggy mass that air cannot penetrate, leading to anaerobic conditions and a slowing-down of the whole process. The most common means of countering this is to keep the texture open and accessible to air by the addition of other materials, usually dry and granular or fibrous. These are called bulking agents or SOAK, typical materials being sawdust, chopped straw or bracken, earth, sand, peat or previously-harvested compost (see Chapter Four for more details on soak materials). Soak can mop up the excess moisture which clogs the pores within the material and prevents air getting in. It also provides rigid elements that maintain open spaces within the composting mass. Soak is useful (and essential in many systems), but it adds to the volume of composting material, which usually means that the minimum size of the chamber is too large to fit into an ordinary house without substantial rebuilding. This 'size' issue occupies a central place in the world of dry toilets.

There are other ways to improve the air supply apart from adding soak. Some dry toilets use hollow bars or grilles of various kinds to break up wet material into smaller pieces (see Figure 3.3). In other cases air is drawn though the unit by fans. In some systems – especially in warm climates – vigorous decomposer animals such as worms are able to cope with quite large accumulations of waterlogged stuff, opening it up and preventing the development of anaerobic conditions.

Temperature

Generally the decomposer organisms operate faster if they are warmer, so decomposition will happen more quickly at higher temperatures. Aerobic breakdown itself generates heat but in most natural situations this is rapidly dissipated and has little effect on the temperature. If however heat *is* generated faster than it can dissipate, the temperature rises and the process speeds up, generating even more heat. The system can bootstrap itself up to around 70°C, and this is what happens by design in carefully made compost heaps and industrial compost processes. It is known as

Fig. 3.3

Fig. 3.3 Aeration bars in a composting toilet chamber. They have an inverted U or V cross section so the channels cannot get clogged by material falling from above; here you can see two attached to a support bar.

THERMOPHILIC (heat loving) composting.

Thermophilic composting is naturally fast and in theory can kill all the pathogens in toilet wastes. The resulting compost will have lost a lot of its organic matter and be very compact. This is an advantage in terms of the size of the unit.

However, very few composting toilets achieve truly thermophilic conditions. Instead they use an aerobic-but-cool process sometimes called MOULDERING, rather like what happens on a forest floor. Mouldering involves a very wide range of decomposer organisms, particularly invertebrates such as worms, woodlice, mites and springtails. The compost may be a long time coming, but it is often of better quality for use as a growing medium than thermophilic compost.

In general, the warmer the compost the quicker it will break down and the smaller your unit can be for a given rate of use. Sources of heat can be internal or external. Internal heat from aerobic breakdown may not be enough to reach thermophilic conditions but is still worth conserving. Therefore it is helpful (though in practice rare) to insulate the composting chamber as far as possible. External sources of heat can be simply from the natural air temperature or from a heated building. So for example if you are designing or specifying a compost toilet for summer use only, or in a permanently warm climate, or in a heated building, it can be smaller than one for all-year use in an unheated building in a cold climate, all other things being equal.

Another alternative is to provide additional heat through heating-elements in the chamber. This will not in itself create aerobic conditions, but could speed up mouldering if it is not *too* hot, and could keep things going in cold weather. However, systems with heating-elements are usually designed for evaporating excess water rather than accelerated composting, and they often sterilise the decomposer organisms through very high temperatures and desiccation (see DEWATERING TOILETS, Chapter Four).

Moisture content

This factor is linked to aeration in that oxygen diffuses very slowly through water. A waterlogged compost mass will quickly become anaerobic and smelly. A dry toilet can become waterlogged if too much moisture, usually urine, goes in too fast. Gruesome stories of 'dry' toilets overflowing after big parties are a staple of alternative toilet folklore. On the other hand, all organisms need a certain amount of water to function, so if the material in the chamber becomes too dry the compost process stalls but it does not smell. This is done deliberately in the case of de-watering toilets, whose aim is simply to get rid of the water which makes up over 90% of toilet wastes. Biologically not much happens, but the volume is drastically reduced and these units can therefore be extremely compact and small enough to fit into a bathroom (see Chapter Five for a review of a typical de-watering toilet).

With TRUE COMPOSTING TOILETS a balance has to be struck. Excess moisture can be controlled by
   • evaporation (with or without electrical assistance)
   • a drain
   • a sump under the unit pumped out from time to time
   • diverting liquids before they get into the body of the unit
   • mopping up by soak material.

These options are all discussed in the next chapter. Getting the moisture content just right can be tricky because households differ greatly in their habits, and it is hard to find out what is going on in the middle of the heap. In the end it is a matter of experience. In general if there is soak material and a drain the system will not become too wet, although it might become too dry as we have experienced with softwood sawdust used over-liberally by first-time users.

Carbon to nitrogen (C:N) ratio

This is an important dimension in all composting. In Figure 3.2 we see carbon as carbon dioxide, while nitrogen is one of the minerals. At the top of the diagram carbon and nitrogen are both present in organic matter in different proportions depending on what sort of matter it is. The breakdown process on the right of the diagram cannot operate with no nitrogen at all, but only about 3% is needed – i.e. a ratio to carbon of about 1:30. If there is much less nitrogen than this the decomposers have trouble with their proteins and nucleic acids and the process slows down; if there is more than this the excess nitrogen is released as oxides or more commonly AMMONIA. Loss of nitrogen to the air might actually be an advantage in cases where the compost is not destined for actual use, but generally compost toilet users would prefer to keep their nitrogen as a fertilizer. A more serious effect of too much nitrogen is that ammonia is toxic to most organisms and could adversely affect the decomposer community. Ammonia is also extremely smelly, in fact the commonest component of toilet smells.

Mixed urine and faeces have a C:N ratio of about 5:1 and they smell as bad as theory predicts. More carbon is needed, and this is generally provided in the form of a high-carbon soak such as sawdust, paper, recycled paper mill sludge (RPMS) or chopped straw. These also serve to keep the texture of the heap open. Ideally the soak materials will break down at exactly the same rate as the toilet wastes, and this true of straw and paper. Joseph Jenkins in *The Humanure Handbook*[1] reports that thermophilic composting works very well with hardwood sawdust, but our experience with cool, mouldering processes has been that the *softwood* sawdust, freely available in Britain, does not break down completely for many years, even though the faeces and paper are completely decomposed. Its benefit is that is smells nice and is pleasant to handle.

Part of the equation, then, is how *accessible* to the decomposer organisms the sources of carbon and nitrogen are. There is plenty of highly soluble nitrogen in very available forms in toilet wastes. From a decomposer's point of view faeces can be regarded as a kind of high-quality pre-digested *pâté de foie*, delicious but if anything a little too rich and needing some nice carbohydrates (equivalent to, say, water-biscuits) to go with it. Wood is generally not very good, but straw or paper make excellent water-biscuits. Straw is a little on the coarse side and is better if chopped (a garden shredder does the job well). Paper is probably best of all, and if paper towels are used for hand drying they should be dropped into the toilet chamber after use, as should toilet roll spindles and any newspaper used to clean the pedestal. Crumpled or balled paper or cardboard of any kind can also be used, but only in single layers. Whole newspapers or magazines are not suitable. There is no problem with printing ink toxicity these days.

RPMS, the sludge left over after recycling paper, is another interesting 'new' material[3]. We have found this makes an excellent soak material in dry toilets, although being 50% clay it does not reduce in volume much. It is probably best used in combination with other materials, but we are not yet in a position to offer a magic formula.

Soak materials are discussed further in Chapter Four. (See page 62.)

Turning

The texture of the mix can also be important on account of the vastly different sizes and methods of feeding of the various decomposer organisms. A tiny immobile organism might quickly exhaust a local supply of carbon or nitrogen and be unable to reach the next bit. For this reason mixing, agitating or 'turning' the pile is invariably beneficial, similar to poking a sluggish fire. Some composting toilet systems include turning or agitation features. In other systems it is the larger decomposer organisms that do the mixing. They do this partly by actually eating and digesting the material, making it accessible to smaller organisms, and partly by their gross activity, making burrows and passageways and heaving material about. This activity also serves to aerate the pile.

Special organisms in the system

In general there will be a wide range of decomposer organisms naturally present in a composting toilet, mostly bacteria and fungi because they are present everywhere. Larger decomposer organisms such as worms are not strictly necessary, but are a great asset if the process is a long cool one, and they are strongly recommended. In a completely enclosed toilet system it will be difficult for these larger decomposers to find their way in, so we suggest putting as many as you can into a new system, plus a spadeful of ordinary garden compost to provide a wide range of smaller decomposers. In the case of CONTINUOUS systems, once the ecosystem has settled down there is no need for further intervention. In BATCH systems (see Chapter Four) it is helpful to seed a new batch with finished compost simply by leaving some of the old stuff in. Generally the best of the large decomposers is the BRANDLING WORM *Eisenia foetida*, common in gardens but also available from fishing tackle shops. A system with a healthy population of these worms (not earthworms) usually works without trouble.

The complex ecosystem in the unit actually 'learns' to deal with the kinds of wastes it normally receives and the process will improve over time. Sometimes there is a rocky start but usually a system will settle down within a few months. The proportions of active organisms may well change during the course of the process, but it will be drawing from an ever-present pool of potential partic15ipants which, like actors, come on when it's their turn. Once they have learned their lines they rarely miss a cue.

Toxic materials and other unfavourable conditions

Poisons, detergents or disinfectants, not surprisingly, can severely affect the function of a biological toilet. Some types of soak material may also affect the decomposers adversely, notably ashes (either coal or wood) which are extremely salty and alkaline. One possible exception is chemical fly-strip which (if necessary) can be used to control flies in the chamber without affecting either the humans in the bathroom or the decomposers in the compost mass.

CONCLUDING REMARKS

The orthodox biology of decomposition helps to make sense of what is happening in compost toilets but so far has not led to a definitive body of practice. Sometimes things work when they shouldn't and fail when they should, but on the whole we get better results if we follow the rules. In the next chapter we will see how the biological principles combine with other design constraints in practical systems.

Chapter Four
Designing Dry Toilets

This is a long chapter containing details of the physical design and operation of dry toilet systems. It should help you decide whether any of these systems could suit your situation and where modifications might be made. It might also help with trouble-shooting existing systems, or suggest improvements. There are three sections:

1. design principles
2. compact toilet units
3. 'true' composting toilets.

DESIGN PRINCIPLES

The WC, being simply a collecting device, is very compact, and bathrooms are arranged accordingly. But a toilet unit which must both collect *and* process material tends to be bigger than a WC, sometimes much bigger, especially if the process is slow and requires the addition of extra material. Therefore it might not fit a pre-existing space. There are three logical alternatives to this problem, each giving rise to a class of dry toilet systems:

1 We can remove the material from the chamber before it is fully processed, and treat it elsewhere. This leads to the class we call BUCKET TOILETS (Figure 4.1a)

2 We can try to reduce the volume by evaporating the water which makes up 90% of the waste. This is done by electrical heaters and fans, which also serve to pasteurise the waste. This is the class called DE-WATERING TOILETS (Figure 4.1b)

3 We can accept the difficulty and try to deal with it in various ways, for example:

Fig. 4.1a Bucket Toilet.

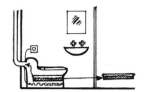

Fig. 4.1b De-Watering Toilet.

Fig. 4.1c Composting Toilet.

The arrows in the diagrams above show the relative volumes of waste that need to be removed per year from each type of system.

- extend the bathroom
- install a chute into a processing chamber on a lower floor, basement or UNDERCROFT
- in the case of a new building integrate the toilet system into the design
- create a separate dedicated structure
- think again how small a composting chamber can be for a given use

These various options lead to the class called COMPOSTING TOILETS, (Figure 4.1c).

Each category has its benefits and disadvantages, and real examples of each are reviewed in Chapter Five. The first two categories – bucket and de-watering toilets – retain the compactness of the WC and can be easily installed in small spaces without a major rebuild, but with characteristic disadvantages such as greater maintenance, high power-consumption and less robust performance. The second two categories – dewatering and composting toilets – treat the toilet wastes IN SITU, that is, in the body of the unit. This is an important distinction. The advantages of *in situ* treatment are that

- no material is handled until it is fully hygienic
- handling is infrequent
- timing is not crucial.

In the case of bucket toilets material is processed remotely from the toilet receptacle – EX SITU[1]. With *ex situ* systems, the treatment process itself might be very similar but the material has to be transported from the collection point to the treatment point, which generally entails frequent handling of material that is not fully treated, often with critical timing, failing which serious hygiene problems can arise. On the other hand with *ex situ* processing we might be freer to arrange things to optimise the composting process.

The three categories are not mutually exclusive, and hybrids are possible. For example, moderate electric heating and fans can be used to speed up composting rather than to desiccate the material, thus reducing the required size. Privies were (and are) often mixed cases. There is also a special *ex situ* case in which a flush toilet can be used and the solids rapidly separated and composted, and here no handling of untreated material is involved. Some regard this as the Holy Grail of on-site treatment (see 'Rapid-Separation Systems' later in this chapter).

There are some important design factors that apply to all three classes. They have to do with *quality* and *performance*, and relate strongly to the Porcelain Standard – that set by the WC in a well-appointed bathroom (see Chapter One). There is a very large difference in 'quality' between the crudest DIY bucket toilets and the most sophisticated power-assisted commercial models. There is also a large difference in cost, and it is broadly true in this field as in others that you get what you pay for. 'Quality' in this context has many aspects, for example:

• **Perceived gentility:** Do you feel comfortable with the system? Are you embarrassed at the prospect of guests using it? Does it look good at first sight? Does it smell?

• **Ease of use:** How quickly can users (in the 'bums-on' sense) learn to operate the system? Immediately? Only after a few uses? Over a long time? Does it remain awkward even after much experience?

• **Ease of maintenance:** How often is routine maintenance required, and how long does it take? Is some of the maintenance unpleasant or tedious? Are there any special skills and are they easily acquired?

• **Reliability in routine use:** How likely is it to go wrong even if correctly used?

- **Pattern of typical faults:** What are the characteristic weak points of the system? Are they easily tolerated or corrected, or are they more serious? What is the worst case? If the system totally breaks down is it merely inconvenient or a total catastrophe?
- **Robustness against misuse:** What happens if it is *not* correctly used? Is it fragile and easily disturbed or can it stand occasional abuse and recover from it?
- **Sturdiness of design and construction:** Is it built to last? does it weather well?

In principle these items can be used as a checklist to evaluate a prospective system, but unfortunately in the current state of the art this cannot really be done without 'horse's mouth' opinions from actual users, hence the case studies presented in Chapter Five. Even if all the technicalities are sorted out, we must emphasise the importance of the human dimension. *You've got to love your toilet.* Regular care, attention to detail and a common-sense approach can make the simplest system pleasant and successful, while over-fastidious tastes combined with neglect can turn even the fanciest system into a nightmare.

COMPACT DRY TOILET UNITS

In this section we shall discuss systems in which the pedestal is small enough to fit into an ordinary bathroom or outhouse. They fall into two groups already mentioned at the beginning of this chapter, plus two special cases:

- a. Bucket toilets
- b. De-watering toilets
- c. Rapid-separation systems
- d. Privies

Bucket toilets:

Moveable sewage containers (from chamber-pots to actual buckets) were common in the days of 'night-soil' collection (Figures 4.2a/b, 4.3 and 4.4). Today they come in the form of chemical toilets for camping, emergency situations, and caravans. Their function is to provide a reasonably hygienic collection

Fig. 4.2a Bedroom commode with seat, cunningly disguised as an ordinary chair. Fig. 4.2b With seat removed, revealing snugly-fitting chamber pot.

Fig 4.3 Bucket toilet container. This ceramic one came from a school in mid-Wales. The open back rested against the wall of a small corridor through which the buckets could be retrieved. The seats must have been rather cold in the winter. Fig 4.4 Old fashioned galvanised chemical toilet.

system for sewage materials to be treated elsewhere. We can distinguish wet (i.e., chemical) and dry varieties.

Chemical Toilets

Although it does offer the opportunity to deposit wastes into a liquid medium, the chemical toilet cannot be described as an attractive solution. The chemical disinfectants generally smell unpleasant, and incur a recurrent cost. The resulting turgid stew with its bobbing dumplings climbs remorselessly up the container towards the user's bottom. Those responsible for emptying vie

Fig. 4.5 Removing the cassette from the pedestal and emptying the cassette through a fitted spout. (© Thetford Services).

with each other to leave it one more day, but the longer it is left the greater the chance of getting a good gollop down your leg when you finally get round to it. The bucket usually has a handle to make things easier, but is hard for one person – or even two – to carry without spilling anything.

Old-fashioned galvanised 'Elsans' (Figure 4.4) with wooden lids are being replaced by all-plastic models, but these are no easier to carry. Generally chemical toilets are emptied into the nearest access to the sewer system – specially provided at campsites but often a regular WC – with many opportunities for slips and spills. Otherwise the contents are often poured into a pit, which does little harm on a small scale but is not to be encouraged. The chemicals themselves are not particularly hazardous or persistent, and the entire contents can be composted, but we would not recommend putting it on compost destined for food production. The risks are very small but it is good practice to keep sewage materials separate from other composting facilities. (See Chapter Nine.)

On the positive side there is a new generation of very compact chemical toilets, generally for use in camper vans and caravans. These have removable cassettes which are much handier, can be thoroughly sealed, and are designed to be easily discharged into a normal WC (Figure 4.5).

Dry Bucket toilets

Alternatively, bucket toilets can use no water at all, replacing the liquid and chemicals with a dry SOAK material which is added after each use. Soak is an important aspect of many alternative systems and is discussed at length later

in this chapter. In dry bucket toilets soak is crucial. It covers the sewage solids, excludes flies, reduces smells, and provides a cosmetic veil. It also soaks up surplus liquids.

Generally these toilets are about the same size as a standard chemical toilet, weighing somewhat less to carry, depending on the type of soak. DIY systems might be as simple as a 25 litre plastic container with a suitable seat (Figure 4.6). The container can be removed bodily (e.g., figures 4.6, 4.8a), lined with a removable sack (Figure 5.2a&b), or may enclose one or more rigid containers that can be removed (Figure 5.3b). Other design choices involve moisture control, venting, 'peak knocking' and automating the application of soak.

Moisture control can be a problem if the toilets are used like an ordinary WC to receive both liquid and solid wastes. Some bucket-type systems with watertight containers just accept this. Others feature a drain at the bottom which must be piped out either into the ground or a collecting vessel at a lower level. This pipe needs to be disconnected and reconnected each time the container is

Fig. 4.6 Simple DIY bucket toilet using a plastic container. (© Joseph Jenkins).

Fig. 4.7 Tara Ekomatic (Finland). Specified for outdoor use, it has a single polyethylene container with a drain, vent and automatic soak dispenser giving the feeling of 'flushing' (© Tara Composters).

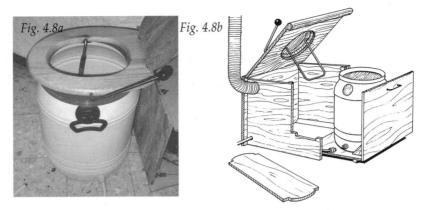

Fig. 4.8a 'Mini-compact composter' developed in the Netherlands. Features include standard (therefore cheap) container, filtered drain, vent and a peak-knocker with very satisfying positive action. Here you can see the peak-knocker (see page 37) mounted through the seat, one of the carring handles and the drain tube. Fig. 4.8b shows a more elaborate arrangement with the container enclosed in a box and mounted on a wheeled trolley. A removable footrest fits onto the front of the box. Complications include disconnecting the drain and vent pipes and dealing with a cacky peak-knocker (© De Twaalf Ambachten).

emptied – a significant and potentially messy extra chore. Furthermore, liquid will remain in the container just below the drain level and is likely to dribble during transport and emptying. Solutions to this problem include

a) Providing alternative facilities for urination and insisting that the unit only receives solids (and small amounts of 'incidental' urine). The drain has only an emergency function. The Mini-Compact Composter developed by the Twaalf Ambachten research group in the Netherlands illustrates this approach (see Figure 4.8a&b).

b) Draining directly into an outer container through a piped drain connection. An example is the Biolet NE, reviewed in Chapter Five. In principle this avoids the need for disconnecting but risks a permanent residue of foetid liquid in the outer container.

c) Providing an integral urine-separating bowl. This the solution adopted by the Swedish Septum and Separett units, also reviewed in Chapter Five.

Venting In cheap-and-cheerful models there is no vent – as with the traditional chemical toilet or the classical privy. These are inclined to be too smelly for bathrooms but are usually OK in outhouses, especially if a pleasant-smelling soak is used, such as fresh sawdust. In the more sophisticated models a vent is provided to carry odours out of the immediate vicinity of the toilet. Vents for bucket systems are usually unpowered, but a small fan will make them more effective.

Peak-knocking Toilet solids do not spread themselves efficiently into the corners of a container. They tend to build up into a remarkably steep-sided faecal stalagmite, the tip of which starts to project through the seat long before the container is actually full. This leaves the user with a choice of needlessly frequent emptying, or (as we say in the trade) 'knocking the peak'. This can be done with any simple tool such as trowel, but is not an agreeable task and tends to foul the tool, which then needs cleaning. Advanced systems incorporate a fitted peak-knocking bar which stays inside the unit but can be operated from outside. This is much better for routine users, but the operator will still be confronted with a messy bar on emptying (e.g Figures 4.8b, 5.3b)

Soak Soak materials are discussed at length later in this chapter. Note however that an automatic soak dispenser is featured in certain commercial models. The Tara Ekomatic, for example, has a hopper looking reassuringly like an ordinary cistern, and a handle which when operated flings soak into the chamber. The whole operation feels like the normal flushing ritual, a pleasing aspect of the design. It is surprising the idea has not been more widely taken up (see Figure 4.7).

***Ex situ* treatment of toilet wastes** The bucket toilet is the *collection* part of the system, and the treatment of the wastes must be carried out elsewhere. In principle this is no different from any other composting process, except that it contains potentially pathogenic material. This means that it should be separate from other composting systems destined to fertilise edible crops, and should be secure against rodents.

In most circumstances it is best to have two containers, one to be filling up while the other is 'doing', to ensure there is no mixing between fresh and processed material. The size depends on how

Fig. 4.9 Milko compost bin. The base has holes large enough to allow drainage of liquid and decomposer access, but too small for rodents.

Fig. 4.10 Tyre stack compost bin. This looks scruffy but is effective and costs nothing. It can be built up to six or seven tyres before getting unstable. It is easy to unstack for recovering the finished product. Here the top tyre uses the complete rim as a heavy lid, with a rock weight just to make sure. Lorry tyres give more volume.

much material you expect to produce (including soak) and a little experience will quickly give you a rough idea. Ordinary commercial compost containers will do perfectly well as long as they are fully contained, with a lid and base. Simple conical or 'Dalek' types such as the Rotol or Compostabin are small but so cheap it is feasible to have several. They should be sited on plain soil. If there is likely to be a rodent problem a steel grille can be placed underneath them with half-inch mesh size. The 'Milko' is a 'Dalek' which comes with its own rodent-excluding base (Figure 4.9).

For determined DIYers we have found that used car or lorry tyres are ideal. They can stack up to five feet and it's always easy to start another stack. The volume will diminish as the compost matures, so tyres can be transferred from an old to a new pile as it builds up. The steel banding in tyres makes it impossible for rats to gnaw their way in (use radials). The base should be on the soil, with a layer of steel mesh if there's likely to be a rat problem, and there should be a secure lid – an orphan dustbin lid will often fit, but a sturdy board with a heavy rock on it is good enough (Figure 4.10).

With soak materials such as softwood sawdust, RPMS or chopped straw nothing more needs to be done, except perhaps adding water occasionally from the rose of a watering can, or leaving the lid off during a rainstorm: compost seems to like rain. If earth or sand has been used for soak it would be helpful to add some straw, or balls of corrugated cardboard. Wood ash is not recommended as a soak as it is chemically rather violent and can kill off the decomposers.

It is unlikely you will notice any heating of these heaps, but don't worry. The slow and steady mouldering process gets there in the end, with the help of worms and all the other creepy-crawlies. If worms do not appear quickly, put some in.

Box 4.1

Safety Aspects of Composting Toilet Wastes:

The potential dangers in untreated sewage lie in the FAECAL PATHOGENS, mostly bacteria but also protozoans and gut parasites such as hookworm, which could be transmitted back to humans by direct contact, or via flies or rodents. It is logical to suggest that pathogens should be killed as quickly as possible, and for this reason some *ex situ* composters advocate a thermophilic process in which the compost gets STERILISED by the naturally generated heat. This approach is advocated by Joseph Jenkins who describes how to do it in his quirky classic *The Humanure Handbook*.[2] He just piles the stuff on with the rest of the kitchen and garden compost and monitors the temperature to make sure it is high enough. He has been using the resulting compost on vegetables for many years and his family have never had any health problems.

We applaud this achievement, but do not recommend the practice. In British conditions it is too difficult to guarantee that the entire heap will reach the required temperatures. We must use time and care instead.

What are the risks?

We are all directly exposed to faecal contamination in (for example) going to the toilet, having baths and cleaning up babies, and we have learned rules of care and hygiene to minimise risks. Disease organisms are all around us and people with healthy immune systems are well able to defend themselves – probably better as a result of constant low-level exposure. Running an *ex situ* dry toilet requires handling fresh faeces, but in doing so it is unlikely you would get higher exposure than by simply going to the toilet yourself. With common sense and care you can avoid direct contact.

After this stage of operation the health risks decline. The finished compost is likely to be about as pathogenic as garden soil. The chances of pathogens surviving long in any sort of compost heap are small. At CAT for instance, tropical pathogens deliberately introduced to dry toilet compost had nearly all disappeared within a few months. The chances of them surviving further in soil, contaminating food crops and surviving washing and cooking in enough numbers to cause any problems, are very small indeed. The recorded cases of sewage-contaminated food have involved the application of raw sewage effluent directly on salad crops in the tropics, which is just asking for trouble.

Whatever you do, the risks are low – certainly far lower than such celebrated hazards as crossing a busy road. However there is no point in taking unnecessary risks and you might as well follow a few rules of good practice. We would suggest the following rules for composting sewage wastes:

• Keep the sewage compost secure against rodents
• Leave at least one year between the start of composting and use
• Use a batch process with each year's compost kept separate
• Only use the resulting compost for ornamental purposes or tree/bush crops – where there is no possibility of contaminating edible parts
• Don't mix sewage and non-pathogenic compost processes in the garden – keep them separate.

This degree of caution might sound 'wasteful' of good nutrients, but we must remember that sewage solids will only be a fraction of the nutrient flow from the house/garden system: there will be plenty of other, non-hazardous compost for use on edibles – including urine (see Chapter Nine).

In summary, it is probably fair to say that we do not know all the answers but can guarantee safe and effective treatment provided the basic rules are followed.

De-Watering Toilets

Even without water for flushing, toilet wastes are mostly water. Urine is more than 98% water and faeces are more than 70% water. The actual amount of solid matter we excrete is quite small – less than 50kg a year, compared with around half a tonne with all the water included. It is tempting then, and technically possible, to deal with toilet wastes simply by dehydration, and this is the principal method adopted by some commercial dry toilets. One can go even further and *incinerate* the resultant dry matter, reducing it to a few kilos of ash. One US model, no longer produced, was called the 'Destroilet': it makes one wonder how far this energy-intensive approach can go...the nuclear toilet? (Figure 4.11).

De-watering is done by a combination of heating and ventilation, using electrical elements, fans and a vent. There are usually also mechanical stirrers to prevent the build-up of a peak, and to spread the material better for drying.

Fig. 4.11 The ultimate solution to the sewage problem?

Advantages :
- the unit can be very compact, fitting into a small space
- the dried material may also be sterilised by the heat, or at least rendered safe until it is removed
- the quantity of material for removal is relatively small, and can be taken discreetly through the house in a clean container
- the ventilator fan maintains a negative pressure and prevents smells.
- there is usually no need for extra materials – chemicals, soak etc.

Disadvantages:
- an electricity connection is needed
- electricity consumption potentially significant – often the toilet will become the largest-consuming appliance in the house
- they are vulnerable to SHOCK LOADS – there is an upper limit to the rate at which it can accept inputs over a short period
- problems often arise if the unit is not in continual use
- the product may be hygienic when removed, but may not be actually composted and requires further treatment to become stable
- there is a risk of total failure in the event of an extended power-cut

Sometimes such compact electrical toilets are the best and only solution, but in practice users are often dissatisfied. The units are very sensitive to misuse – readily overwhelmed by a serious party, for example. Re-commissioning after a breakdown is not a job for the faint-hearted. A common problem arises when the units are installed in holiday-homes and are left for long periods without use. The de-watering process can sometimes transform a mixture of toilet paper, urine and faeces into a kind of paper *mâché* that coats the innards of the toilet so tenaciously that it is almost impossible to remove. Its strength is so impressive one imagines there could be industrial applications for it (see Chapter Five for a review of one of these systems).

Another practical problem is that because the units are so small and no soak material is used, the most recent deposit will be rather 'in your face' until it is processed. For cosmetic reasons most of these units have a shutter system to hide the contents, which slides back automatically as you sit on the seat (see Figure 5.3a). These shutters are ingenious but sometimes jam. Worse, if the unit has not been emptied or cannot keep up with a bout of heavy use the shutter may foul a protruding item, smearing it about, often in places which are hard to clean without dismantling the whole unit. The shutter is usually operated by the weight of the user on the seat, and this is awkward for conventional male urination. Males using these systems should sit to urinate, but some develop a knack of opening the shutter with one knee resting on the seat while managing the rest of the operation semi-standing. This is a recipe for erratic aim and regular mishaps.

Fig. 4.12 Tray of finished material being removed from a dewatering unit.

Since most of the work of the unit is evaporation, and since most of the liquid comes from urine it greatly improves the performance of these units to collect urine separately if at all possible. This is easier for males but even for females it would be worth making some effort to provide urine-collection facilities (see Chapter Six).

The finished material is usually removed in a tray at the base of the unit and should be attractive and odourless (Figure 4.12). It should also be pasteurised and free of pathogens, so that it can be put into a compost heap, dug into the garden or, if needs be, put into the dustbin or garbage sack for collection. However, in most cases the 'finished' material is not so much compost as dehydrated faeces in suspended animation, and needs proper composting to reach a fully stable condition.

Electricity consumption varies a great deal according to the model and the use it gets. Generally it is similar to a fridge, but may be much less or much more, costing up to 50p a day in electricity. If your purposes in installing such a toilet are environmental (preventing pollution and saving water and nutrients) you have to weigh the impact of its energy consumption against the benefits. In our view it would not usually be a rational choice.

We have perhaps been a little hard on the de-watering toilets, so we should say that under ideal conditions, used with care, they can be quite satisfactory. A system is reviewed in Chapter Five.

Rapid-Separation Systems

This is a relatively new but promising approach. The idea is to keep a WC of some kind and use small amounts of water to transport toilet wastes from the pedestal, then quickly separate the solids and liquids before the liquids are seriously contaminated. This gives solids dry enough for effective composting in a convenient location, plus a liquid effectively of GREYWATER quality. It means that the structure of the bathroom or the building does not need to be distorted to accommodate a large chamber immediately beneath the pedestal – although sometimes the chamber has to be installed awkwardly below ground level.

The advantages of these systems are that:
- they retain the WC type pedestal (usually a low-flush version)
- bathroom plumbing is conventional
- the treatment chamber can be anywhere convenient below the level of the pedestal
- the treatment chamber can be designed to optimise composting, access etc
- the liquids join the greywater treatment system, which must

normally be provided for other household purposes

The disadvantages are that:

• Heights and levels are critical
• They can be expensive
• Some systems only work in warm climates

There are two principal methods for rapid separation:

1) Filtration through the compost mass.

Here the mixed sewage falls onto a composting pile much as in a standard dry toilet, but the liquid drains through to a second compost layer, then a third, leaving behind suspended solids and emerging with a level of contamination similar to greywater. This type, represented by the DOWMUS 'biolytic filter', works well in the warm climates of Australia[3]. Unfortunately (so far) nobody has succeeded in reproducing this success in cool Britannia, although a modified version is described in Chapter Five, and see also Figure 4.17.

2) Centrifugal/Coanda effect.

Here the mixed sewage enters a specially-designed spiral structure rather like an egg timer with a hole through the middle. Solids fall through the hole into the composting chamber while liquids circulate centrifugally, clinging to the sides of the structure until they reach the outflow pipe. There are no moving parts. Again the effluent liquid is about greywater quality, although an ultraviolet unit is sometimes recommended to kill pathogens. The chamber can be of almost any design and is essentially the same as a composting toilet chamber, so these systems represent hybrids between conventional and composting systems, with some of the advantages and disadvantages of both.

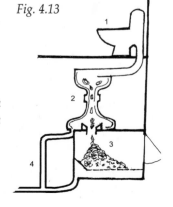

Fig. 4.13

Fig. 4.13 The Aquatron rapid-separation system (Sweden). The system has four components: 1. a low-flush or urine-separating toilet, 2. the centrifugal separating unit, 3. the composting chamber, 4. liquid treatment system. Compare figure 5.7a&b.

This type is represented by the 'Aquatron' which *does* work in cold climates (Figure 4.13), and a working system is described in Chapter Five.

Box 4.2

Privies:

Before the WC, there was the privy, still found in rural areas. Essentially a privy is a chamber or hole in the ground surmounted by a seat of some kind, and is usually out of doors in a small building. Two-hole or even three-hole models were common. After use it was the practice to shovel in a small amount of earth, ashes, lime or other loose material to deter flies and reduce smells, and some privies had hoppers with automatic delivery systems, known as an 'earth closet'. When full, the contents could be physically dug out or a new hole made and the lightweight structure moved to the new location. It has been suggested that the excavated material was often put into trenches in the garden, and that this was the origin of the tradition of 'double digging'. It may account for the very rich dark soils in many older gardens. Where

Fig. 4.14

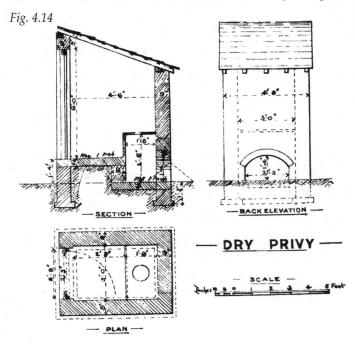

Fig. 4.14 Charles Richardson's plan for his dry privy.

still in use, most privies have been converted to bucket toilets of one kind or another. One particular design came close to the spirit of modern compost toilets, and could be worth reconsidering. Proposed by Charles Richardson in 1886, this consisted of a brick chamber with a floor sloping out through an arched opening at the back onto a soil bed, which was banked up with soil. Soil or soak material was used to cover fresh material in the privy, but everything could be removed from the outside. Richardson was a firm advocate of keeping things dry:

"The Dry Privy requires no looking after, and is never offensive; all that it requires is that it should be emptied once in six months or so, and this is done without trouble in five minutes, when the earth and droppings are shovelled out on the level and mixed with a little more earth, after which a barrow full of fresh earth is tipped against the archway, and that is all that is wanted. If what is taken out is left in a heap for two or three weeks it becomes a valuable manure for the garden.

Old fashioned privies, instead of having the floor raised two steps above the surface usually have cess-pits dig into the ground; these are a mistake, for they hold water, and thus form Sewage, which makes the privy very offensive and sometimes the cause of the propagation of fevers round about them; besides making the emptying very difficult and offensive. But the evils of these are as nothing compared with those of the water-closet."

In some places the privy structure was simply placed over a running stream, and we have seen properties with no other toilet facilities archly described by estate agents as having 'waterborne sanitation'! Outside Europe there is an even larger range of types, and many varieties are described in the sanitation literature for developing countries[4] not all of which would impress the UK public health authorities (e.g. Figure 4.15).

For those with a taste for it, there is an entertaining sub-literary genre of European and American privy lore – a lode of *double entendre* and scatological anecdotes[5].

Fig. 4.15 Pig privy from Goa, India.

REAL COMPOSTING TOILETS

Of all the varieties of alternative toilets described in this book, genuine *in situ* composting toilet systems are usually the most reliable where circumstances permit them to be installed. We shall therefore go into more detail in this section. Rather than describe toilets one by one it is probably more enlightening to go through the design problems and functional elements they all share to show the potential variety of solutions. Here we are treating readers as if they are potential designers of composting toilets. Admittedly, this will not often be the case, but even if you are buying ready-made systems there is a certain element of pick 'n mix, and an understanding of the principles will help make the right choices. It does not make for easy reading, so if you merely want some general impressions, skip the rest of this chapter and look at actual examples in Chapter Five.

Segregating old and new material

It takes time. But fresh material is constantly arriving, potentially mixing with material already processed. If we want to guarantee that only fully processed compost is removed for further use, it is vital to keep the old separate from the new.This can be done either on a *continuous* basis – the old material being pushed continuously along or down by the new; or on a *batch* basis where material is segregated into different compartments according to age. The same problem – and the same choice – exists with *ex situ* systems.

Continuous processing:

The classic continuous-process design has a sloping chamber in which older material is gradually pushed down and sideways. The layout, or a baffle, may prevent fresh material getting out of sequence (Figure 4.16). Some practitioners are sceptical about the effectiveness of the sloping base, and recommend a simpler box-like chamber in which material needs occasional raking towards the exit (Figure 4.17, see also Figures 5.9 and 5.10).

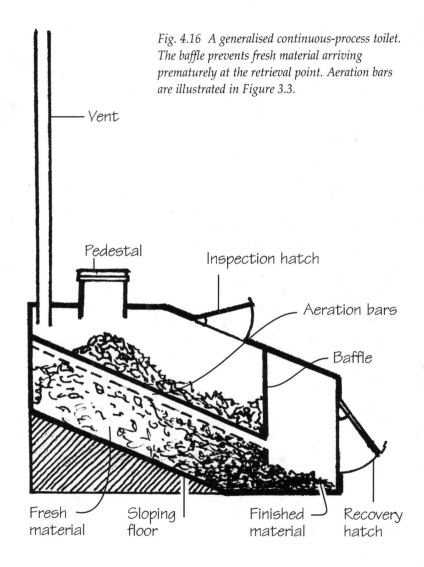

Fig. 4.16 A generalised continuous-process toilet. The baffle prevents fresh material arriving prematurely at the retrieval point. Aeration bars are illustrated in Figure 3.3.

Vent

Pedestal

Inspection hatch

Aeration bars

Baffle

Fresh material

Sloping floor

Finished material

Recovery hatch

Fig. 4.17 A classic scandinavian-type continuous-process compost toilet. The arrangement takes advantage of a change in level. The front part of the base slopes at about 40°. There is a port for inspection and peak-knocking on the top side. Material is removed through a door at the bottom rear end. There is no drain, and in use this system always had a layer of liquid in the bottom.

Fig. 4.18 A 'Euro-Dowmus' system under construction. The composting chamber can be seen beneath the floor level, with the door for peak-knocking and retrieval. There is a very slight slope towards the door. See Chapter Five for a case study.

Batch processing:

The classic batch design is the twin-vault in which two chambers are used alternately (Figure 4.19 and Appendix One). When one chamber is full the system switches to the other, which usually involves moving the entire pedestal. Alternatively the chambers can move (Figure 4.20). An ingenious Dutch design achieves the effect by rotating the whole unit around a horizontal axis, which also serves to agitate the compost (Figure 4.21).

Fig. 4.19

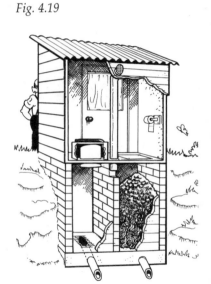

Fig. 4.20

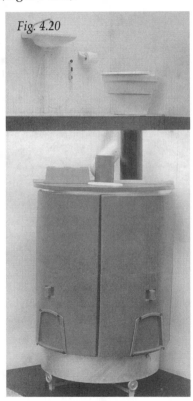

Fig. 4.19 A twin-vault system. In this illustration the full chamber is on the right, now sealed with a floor plate. The pedestal has been moved to the new, empty chamber.

Fig. 4.20 A carousel-type system (Ekolet, Finland). The composting unit, mounted on wheels, has four separate chambers. When one is full it is topped with earth and the whole vessel rotated 90°. (© Ekolet).

Fig. 4.21

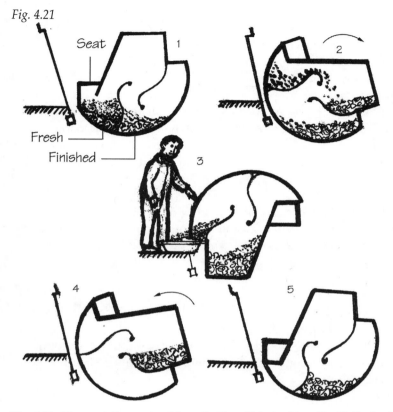

Seat

1

2

Fresh

Finished

3

4

5

Fig. 4.21 'Compact Composteur' from De Twaalf Ambachten, The Netherlands. The unit is made of polypropylene and mounted on a central axis. It is turned by a ratchet to produce the separation/agitation/emptying sequence illustrated here. 4.21(5) Fresh material now in rear chamber.

Drainage

There is potentially a great deal of water in a dry toilet system because:

- toilet wastes are largely water
- water is generated in waste decomposition
- there is always a possibility of 'shock loads' of urine
- water from a wash-basin may be run into the chamber

For these reasons a drain is often provided to remove surplus water. It needs to drain *to* somewhere, but this is often problematic if the compost chamber is already in a basement or dug into the ground: there is nowhere lower for the water to go. In this case you must either collect it in a suitable container and remove it for treatment elsewhere, or pump it out. Some of the fancier models have a specially designed sump for collecting liquid, either with a gauge to tell you when it is full, or a switch to turn on the pump automatically. The amount and quality of the liquid is variable, depending on the patterns of use and the type of soak material. Not surprisingly it is brown in colour, but usually it does not smell, being less unpleasant than stale urine. It might well contain pathogens but not in alarming concentrations. It can be fed into the greywater system or, diluted at least fivefold, used to water non-edible plants. Where suitable conditions exist it is allowed simply to drain away into the ground, being about as environmentally dangerous as a cow-pat (see review of Clivus Multrum system in Chapter Five).

Compost toilets built from scratch in a remote site are usually built onto a concrete slab with drainage channels (Figure 4.22) but from a biological and practical viewpoint the best solution is for the bottom of the chamber to be open to bare soil. This guarantees effective drainage and a steady two-way traffic of decomposer organisms, although it might be queried by Public Health in some circumstances.

Fig. 4.22 DIY toilets such as twin-vaults are commonly built on a concrete slab into which drainage elements are incorporated. Two possible systems are illustrated here: a grille with tube, or simple runnels.

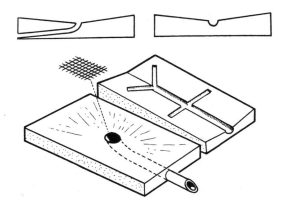

Dry-toilet users often find that in practice there is no surplus liquid at all. We are approaching a point at which we can design chambers without any drainage provided certain other conditions are met, such as urine-separation, which is discussed next.

Urine Separation

In household WCs, urine and faeces disappear indiscriminately down the pan. This has advantages in terms of cost, simplicity, and ease of use, so dry toilets have tended to follow suit without giving the matter much thought. But now we are starting to think again, for several reasons:

- optimum treatment processes for urine and faeces are often different
- unpredictable inputs of urine can disturb the moisture balance
- the saltiness and ammonia produced by urine can be toxic to decomposer organisms
- the odours produced by urine get stronger over time, while those of faeces diminish
- jets of urine can wash away soak, exposing faeces to flies and causing smells
- urine is pathogen-free and a richer source of nutrients than faeces – mixing the two contaminates the urine and restricts its applications.

For such reasons it is usually advisable to minimise the amount of urine entering the chamber. This does not need to be taken to extremes: small amounts of urine in the chamber will not be a problem. In practice, how is urine-separation achieved?

Urinals:

One perfectly straightforward method, particularly suitable for public toilets, is to provide urinals for male users. This delivers another bonus in odour reduction. Most of the odours in dry toilets seem to arise from stray male urine, since the pedestal typically offers a small, distant target with a wide rim often made of wood, which readily soaks up stray urine (Figure 4.23). Men ought to sit of course, but don't unless forced (Figure 4.24). The practical alternative to this is to offer a urinal nearby, with stern notices, as we have done successfully in one dry toilet at CAT (Figure 4.25). A

Fig. 4.23

Fig. 4.23 DIY wooden pedestal. This is very low, with a wide lip at the front. Poor targeting and dribbles from standing urinators are almost inevitable. The ribbon is not a permanent feature!
Fig. 4.24 A clever Swedish idea to prevent standing urination.
Fig. 4.25 Sign behind pedestal ot twin-vault system at C.A.T.

Fig. 4.24

Fig. 4.25

> **GENTLEMEN!**
> **This is a sitting-only toilet.**
> **If you want a pee please use the**
> **waterless urinal behind you.**
> **Thank you.**

urinal offers a much larger target, is more easily cleaned, and of course separates urine. The urinals do not need flushing (see Chapter Six).

Urine traps:

An alternative arrangement – not recommended for public toilets – is to have a urine-collecting trap in the pedestal or the toilet chamber. In principle this could apply across the spectrum of toilet types including WC's, bucket toilets, de-watering toilets and composting toilets. (See Chapter Five for some examples.) How does this work? Anatomically, for both males and females, urine tends to be projected forward and faeces straight down or slightly back, so a bowl at the front should catch most of the urine. In practice we have found this is not always the case because anatomies differ – particularly among women. If a small amount of urine falls into the main chamber that is not a problem but getting faeces into the urine collection bowl certainly is. It can happen with smaller children using 'adaptor seats' or perched on the edge of the pedestal reading *The Beano*. To minimise this problem the main seat should be placed as far back as possible and the collection bowl as far forward as possible, although in most designs there is no room for adjustment. Of course regular users soon learn to operate the system perfectly, but guests may need a few guidelines in the form of friendly notices advising them to sit well back.

Fig. 4.26

Fig. 4.26 Ekologen ES (Sweden). Urine-separating pedestal for compost toilets. It does not strictly need flushing, but a half-pint swish can be delivered automatically or simply by pouring into the urine bowl. (© Nick Grant)

For composting toilets the only commercial urine-separating pedestal is the Swedish Ekologen ES, which combines a collection bowl, a 'black hole' direct drop and an efficient flushing mechanism. This is an excellent compromise between a number of requirements (Figure 4.26).

In systems with a CHUTE (see below) urine is usually projected against the chute side and runs down into the chamber. The chute is usually made of a smooth material that does not absorb liquids and can be easily cleaned. Where there is no chute there is a danger that urine can be projected onto the sides of the chamber, which may absorb it and allow odours to develop. In these cases it is best to install a splash-plate of smooth material, or a half-chute (Figure 4.27a/b).

Fig. 4.27a

Fig. 4.27b

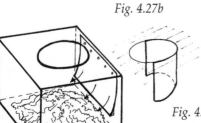

Fig. 4.27a Splash-plate on front of chamber or pedestal, b) Half-chute. Will not get fouled by faeces but deflects urine into compost mass.

If urine is going to be deflected from the walls of a chamber, why not take the opportunity to channel it away completely? Andy Warren of Natural Solutions has carried out pioneering research in this area, and Figure 4.28 shows a logical development of Figure 4.27a, with an ordinary rain gutter running off to a collection point outside the chamber. Figure 4.29 goes even further – a stainless steel plate curved to form an offset gutter that cannot be fouled by falling faeces. Once urine reaches the plate it clings to it by surface tension and can run into the gutter, while falling objects drop straight past into the chamber. At the time of writing this system is under trial.

The separated urine can then be run to a collecting tank for disposal or further use (see Chapter Nine).

Fig. 4.28 Urine collecting gutter viewed through the opening of a compact chamber, designed by Andy Warren. The contents of the chamber would not normally be so conspicuous, but in this illustration are illuminated by the flash.
Fig. 4.29 Urine-collecting plate designed by Andy Warren, removed for a better view. It would normally be mounted vertically, and takes advantage of the fact that urine will run along a receding surface to a gutter which cannot get fouled by faeces. The lip at the top allows for flushing if required.

The Pedestal and Chute

From an everyday point of view the pedestal is the most important part of a toilet system: what most people call 'the toilet'. But we should remind ourselves that the need for a pedestal arises from the Western custom of 'sitting on the toilet'. Most cultures traditionally squat to defecate, so the requirement for something which sticks up out of the floor is not absolute. In the case of bucket and de-watering toilets the pedestal serves important purposes in collecting, storing and processing wastes, but with composting toilets consisting principally of large chambers the pedestal has no particular function. Nevertheless, Western users will continue to demand something of the kind, and the usual pattern is simply to place a pedestal on top of the chamber, as in many examples already illustrated. Sometimes the pedestal is a wooden box topped with a seat and lid, lined with a smooth-sided chute. In other cases pedestal and chute are combined as a self-supporting structure in plastic or ceramic analogous to a WC pedestal. The chute may be extended vertically by several metres to a composting chamber directly below the pedestal. Apart from providing something to sit on, the chute serves to channel toilet wastes into the chamber, provides an easily-cleaned surface, and discreetly obscures the contents of the chamber by cutting out most of the light. There is certainly a dramatic contrast between the 'white pool' of the WC and the 'black hole' of the true compost toilet.

As with any toilet pedestal, WC included, a chute can get fouled. From a hygiene and gentility point of view it is very important to keep the chute clean. Cleaning should be carried out as quickly as possible after the fouling event, and can be done with a domestic spray bottle and an ordinary toilet brush. Newspaper is very effective, and can be simply dropped into the chamber when the operation is complete (see DOWMUS case study, Chapter Five). The chute is usually made of plastic, mostly commonly white but sometimes black. In DIY systems the favoured chute is a white plastic drum of the kind used in home-brewing, with the bottom cut off. This has about the right height and a slight taper. It therefore jams snugly into a circular hole, spans the gap between the opening and the seat, and will often need no further fixing. In systems where the seat switches it is easy to remove and replace on the other side.

Fig. 4.30 Pedestal and chute removed from a DIY compost toilet. Here you can see the pedestal box and tapered chute together, viewed from underneath. The chute would wedge solidly into a circular opening on the top of the chamber. You can also see quite a lot of faecal fouling which if left too long is almost impossible to remove.

Fig. 4.31 'Short sharp chute'. Mimimal fouling risk, easy to clean, but serves to deflect urine and obscure the chamber contents (© Andy Warren).

Fig. 4.32 DOWMUS pedestal (Australia). This ceramic, bell-shaped pedestal is almost an art object. Best cleaned with damp newspaper. Note the absence of pipework.

Figure 4.30 shows that converging chutes, especially long ones, are easily fouled. Better are short chutes such as illustrated in Figure 4.31, and better still bell-shaped chutes which could even be self-supporting. As far as we know there is only one of these commercially available and unfortunately it is made in small quantities in Australia and costs several hundred pounds in the UK. It does however represent a design breakthrough and is made of white sanitary porcelain (Figure 4.32). Having said this, although white is a good conventional colour it can sometimes act as an attractive light-pipe for flies, so functionally a dark-coloured chute is better. The ultimate combined chute/pedestal is probably one made of black, brown or dark grey sanitary porcelain, and perhaps one day these colours may replace peach and avocado as the norm of bathroom fashion.

Fig. 4.33 a)   *b)*   *c)*

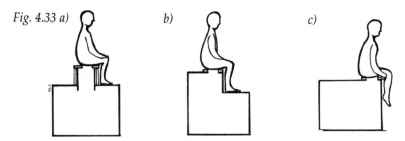

Fig. 4.33 Relationship of chamber, pedestal and chute. 33a) The most common arrangement, with pedestal and chute mounted over the composting chamber, 33b) Chamber with integral bench, 33c) Seat directly on the chamber. This last arrangement saves some height and might allow a modestly-sized chamber to be retro-fitted in an inside bathroom. It usually requires a step and/or footrest.

But do we really need chutes? Figure 4.33 compares the combined chute/pedestal arrangement (4.33a) with other logical possibilities, where material falls directly into the chamber (4.33b and c). If chutes act only as funnels they are bound to get fouled from time to time. The view is gaining ground that chutes should only be used if absolutely necessary and it is better to do without them, using instead systems such as illustrated in Figures 4.27-4.29. (See also Appendix Two.)

The outside of the pedestal also deserves attention. It should be well-sealed, light-proof and fly-proof. According to our experience its main problems arise from stray urine. Every effort should be made to ensure that the toilet is only used in a sitting posture. Occasionally this will fail, so the structure must be easily cleanable. Cleaning is straightforward for plastic or metal but more difficult for wood as it easily absorbs urine. Any wood therefore must be very smooth and carefully varnished with at least three coats. The point where the pedestal reaches the floor is also sensitive, since urine can run down and accumulate in cracks. There must be a clean join, preferably sealed with mastic. It is advisable for the floor of the room around the pedestal to be of an impervious, easily cleaned material such as lino or sealed floor tiling.

The space between the edge of the pedestal and the opening is particularly critical because it receives drips from standing urinators. It should be as narrow as possible and designed to be easily cleaned. This is a common design fault in many DIY toilets we have seen, a wide lip making drips and splashes almost inevitable which, unless cleaned immediately, leads to corrosive-looking stains and a permanent smell of stale urine (Figure 4.23).

A regular WC has a seat and a lid. Both are lifted for standing urination. Many compost toilet pedestals have only a lid, the seat being a hole in the top of the pedestal box. In DIY systems it is important to get a good seal between the lid and the seat to minimise stray odours and the movement of flies. In outhouses this can result in condensation building up just on the edge where you sit, and users would be advised to give the seat a quick wipe with toilet paper before use. This does not happen where the pedestal is in a heated space.

Veiling the Contents

On account of the complex and brittle psychology of toilets (see Chapter One) it is better if you can't see the contents of the compost chamber. Invisibility usually comes naturally to large chambers with their 'black hole', but is a problem with smaller systems. We have already met shutters (see above and Figure 5.3). The Vera 'Waterless' has a clever hemisphere that swivels when you sit on

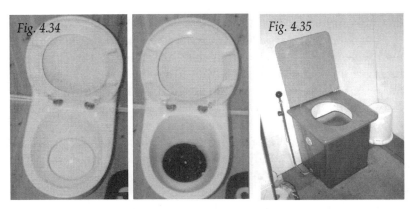

Fig. 4.34 *Vera 'Waterless' pedestal (Norway). The hemispheric device acts as a 'nedsynshinder' which translates as 'that which stops you looking down', a word we could do with in this field.*

Fig. 4.35 *De Twaalf Ambachten Compact Composteur (Netherlands). Here you see the pedestal with lid open and shutter closed. The operating lever is on the left. This can be related to the diagrams of the whole system in Figure 4.20.*

the toilet, forming a cup to receive your contribution. As you get up it swivels again, dropping the contents into a collecting chamber below and presenting a clean convex surface (Figure 4.34). The Compact Composteur features a manually-operated stainless steel plate, operation of which also serves to knock the peak. A clever touch (Figure 4.35).

Peak Knocking

Compost toilets have similar peak-knocking requirements to compact toilets, although timing is usually less critical. This is one of the occasional duties of the owner or operator. It can act as a form of compost-turning and improve the efficiency of the process, and also offer an opportunity to inspect the progress of composting, make adjustments to humidity etc. It is normally done with any rake-like tool. You can make your own out of (for example) a broken shovel-handle (See Figure 4.36).

An ingenious alternative is found in Andy Warren's compact design where a loose riddle bar emerges through a flexible seal, usually at the front. A handle can be fixed onto the end of the bar for leverage whenever peak-knocking is considered necessary (Figure 4.37).

Fig. 4.36

Fig. 4.36 Peak-knocking tool for moderate-sized chambers, made from a broken shovel handle. It can usually live in the chamber without the handle end getting fouled.

Fig. 4.37 Riddle-bar for small composting toilet. The end of the bar stays inside. The outer part is fitted on when peak-knocking is required and gives excellent leverage. In this illustration you can see the footrest characteristic of the Figure 4.33c 'ride on' type of toilet.

If the hole into the chamber from the seat or pedestal is on one side, the peak will build up against one wall. You have to be careful if this is the same wall as the access doors for peak-knocking or emptying.

Vents

Although most privies and the simplest kinds of bucket toilets do not have vents, venting makes a big difference to odour and fly problems. The vent is usually a chimney or tube running from the toilet chamber to a high point outside the building. In most composting chambers the material is at least slightly warmer than the surroundings and this warms the air above it, which tends to rise. If there is no vent this air will come out through the pedestal bringing its odours with it and attracting flies.

Venting can be passive or powered with an electric fan. Passive vents should be generously sized – at least 150mm diameter – to minimise friction and help the air rise quicker. A wind-powered rotating cowl will help the draw (Figure 4.38). Taller vents are generally more effective. They should reach at least 900mm above the highest window of the building. Horizontal sections should be avoided – go straight up if possible.

Fig. 4.38

Powered venting is strongly recommended. The vent-pipe diameter can then be reduced to 100mm. The fan is usually at the bottom of the vent and runs continuously. This maintains a steady negative pressure at the pedestal seat and should result in even less odour than a conventional bathroom. The power rating can be very low – just a few Watts, costing a few pounds a year at mains electricity prices. A rotating cowl is still recommended to prevent occasional back-up gusts from strong winds.

Fig. 4.38 Rotating cowl for vent-pipes.

Flies

Various kinds of flies can breed in the compost chamber and come out through the seat into the room. There are many different kinds, for example fruit flies, which you will get if vegetable wastes are put in the toilet, and fungus gnats which are like midges but do not bite. It is unlikely that any of these flies pose a health hazard, and if they stay in the composting chamber they are a useful part of the decomposer community. Out in the room however they are irritating and cosmetically unpleasant. With a well-functioning vent there are no smells in the room to attract the attentions of flies, especially if the toilet lid fits well. But it is likely that colonies of flies will establish themselves from time to time so it is as well to be prepared.

Most flies move naturally towards a light source in a dark space. This means that if the lid does not fit well any flies in the chamber will be in the pedestal area waiting for their chance to come out. For this reason it is not a good idea to have windows in the room that could allow direct sunlight onto the seat at any time of day. On the other hand the attraction of flies to a light source can be used to draw them *away* from the pedestal. The simplest method is to use the vent, especially in passively vented systems. Ideally the vent should run vertically upwards from the chamber so that light at the top can be clearly seen from the bottom. A metal gauze is placed over the top of the vent to prevent other insects coming in at night, attracted by the smell. Flies then fly up the vent pipe and are trapped near the top. Generally a few canny spiders are on hand to take advantage of the steady supply of food, and this is a good functional arrangement, although the cobwebs need cleaning away from time to time – perhaps once a year.

If the vent cannot be used, an alternative is a simple FLY TRAP made out of a jam jar, invented by the ever-resourceful Andy Warren. This is particularly suitable on wooden pedestals (see Figure 4.39).

If flies are a persistent problem the best method of control is probably an insecticidal strip hung inside the chamber. This might not sound very 'ecological' but it does control flying insects without affecting the other decomposers in the compost mass.

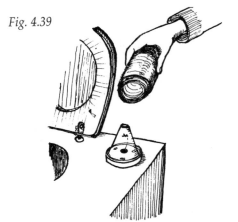

Fig. 4.39

Fig. 4.39 Fly trap designed by Andy Warren. The lid of a screw-top jam jar is drilled with a hole 2-3 mm in diameter, and screwed over a hole in the top of the chamber. A cone of clear plastic sheeting (made from overhead transparency foil) is fitted into the lid and the jar screwed home upside down. It is unscrewed and emptied as required.

Soak

Soaks have been mentioned several times as an important part of most compost toilet systems, but our knowledge about how they work and how best to use them is still rudimentary. In the case of small bucket toilets soak is added after each use for obvious reasons: to cover the last deposit with a cosmetic veil, reduce its smell, prevent flies settling on the fresh material and mop up surplus liquid. This default pattern has been carried over to some larger, more sophisticated systems, perhaps unnecessarily. It is usually soak rather than faeces that occupies most of the space in the chamber, so from the point of view of keeping the size down it is better to use as little soak as possible. Systems have been observed to work with small amounts added only once a week; or only at the start; or even none at all. Where there is good venting and moisture-control the cosmetic aspects of soak are probably unimportant, and biological functions – aeration and a supply of carbon – are more significant. A daily or weekly routine in which 'the operator' adds relatively small amounts of soak might be better than leaving users to add soak indiscriminately.

Where the cosmetic aspects are important there is usually a container with a scoop next to the pedestal. The container, scoop and soak material can be agreeable features of the toilet setting, or just a source of mess and untidiness: attention to design details can be important here.

Table.4.1

Table of common and potential soak materials

——————①—————— ——————②——————

Material	Nice to handle	Smells nice	Covers well	Good for aeration	Good carbon source	Easily available	Cheap or Free	Reduces in volume	Other features
Straw	○	○	▼	✔	✔	○	▼	●	
Chopped straw	●	○	●	✔	✔	▼	▼	●	
Hemp & flax shiv ③	●	○	●	✔	✔	▼	○	●	● ⑤
Softwood sawdust	✔	✔	✔	●	○	●	●	▼	
Hardwood sawdust	✔	●	✔	●	●	▼	○	○	
Waste paper & card	○	○	○	●	✔	✔	✔	✔	
RPMS ④	●	○	●	●	○	▼	○	▼	● ⑤
Garden Compost	●	●	●	●	●	○	○	●	○ ⑥
Leafmould	●	●	●	●	✔	○	●	●	
Peat	●	○	✔	●	●	●	✗	○	▼ ⑦
Soil	●	○	●	●	○	●	●	▼	
Wood Ash	○	○	●	▼	✗	○	●	▼	▼ ⑧

Key: ✔ Very good   ● Good   ○ Moderate   ▼ Poor   ✗ Very poor

Notes:

1 These features are important for bucket toilets and small composters where the material is rather 'in your face', and soak is applied after every use.

2 These features are more important for larger *in-situ* composters where soak might be applied from time to time.

3 Shiv is a fibrous, chaff-like material left over from hemp and flax processing.

4 RPMS is Recycled Papermill Sludge left over from recycling paper, with a texture similar to apple crumble topping. It is at least 50% clay so does not reduce a great deal in volume. It does however combine well with faecal matter and appears to encourage worms. It is technically free but difficult to obtain in retail quantities.

5 It is beneficial to use industrial waste products and improve their value.

6 Although compost works very well as a soak it does become technically 'unclean' and of a lower versatility in the garden than when it started, ie it cannot now be used on edible crops.

7 Peat is a good soak material but a scarce resource with negative environmental implications.

8 Wood ash is not recommended as a soak because it kills most decomposer organisms and inhibits composting.

There is a good variety of potential soak materials (see Table 4.1), although none is perfect. Probably better results could be obtained by mixing different materials, but the number of combinations is large and it will take many years to build up the appropriate body of experience.

Location and access

It is a basic feature of composting toilets that the chambers are large and directly below the pedestal, and this constrains siting. Access to the chamber, required for peak-knocking and removing finished material, must also be considered (Figure 4.40 and Appendix One). There is however a good choice of different arrangements, shown in Figure 4.41. The compact design which fits entirely into a pre-existing bathroom space (Figure 4.41e) is a special case which will only work in certain circumstances. See Appendix Two for further details.

Fig. 4.40

Fig. 4.40 Typical door design for DIY chambers. The top part of the door can be removed for inspection and peak-knocking without half the contents falling out. For emptying, both halves are removed.

Fig. 4.41

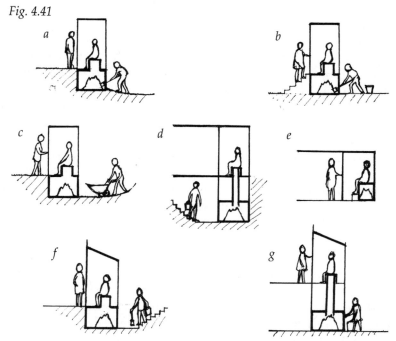

Fig. 4.41 Siting and access for compost toilets. a-c specially built structures; d-e in a building; f-g extensions.

The Surroundings

The user's experience of a dry toilet will depend a great deal on the context. Other people's filth and smells are always more disturbing than our own, so in the case of unfamiliar toilets it is important to pay even more attention to cleanliness and order. Non-toilet features should be as 'normal' and respectable as possible to minimise the shock of the new – unless of course you *want* to shock. This applies particularly strongly in the case of public toilets.

Where a special structure is created to house the toilet we would recommend it be made as large as practical. Even though technically the seat will fit into quite a small space, the ideal would be to have enough room to move around, and to locate a urinal some way from the pedestal. A sink and running water of some kind is strongly recommended. Windows need careful thought so as not to affect actual privacy or provoke fear of its being compromised. It is very nice to sit and look at an agreeable view. If this is not possible, net curtains, frosted glass or clerestory windows can provide light without being overlooked – although glass is not essential in outhouses. Pleasantly painted walls or wallpaper are easily provided and have a strongly positive effect.

Although toilet users do not like to be bossed about, a few coherent instructions and some words of encouragement do not come amiss. If the toilet is likely to be used by many first-timers or the general public it is an advantage to flag it up as experimental and make a feature of its environmental virtues. People actually using a toilet often have the leisure to read a paragraph or two, so you could have a poster on the wall, or perhaps a framed cut-away diagram explaining how the system works. No need to be too grimly serious about it. If you are interested in contributing to the body of experience why not have a log book and a pencil available and ask users to record their impressions?

Until now most true composting toilets have been located in outhouses or extensions. We are probably at the point now where high-quality systems can be incorporated into bathrooms and start to displace WCs (see Appendix Two). The only barrier remaining is lack of public familiarity.

Routine Maintenance

As with any toilets, biological ones need regular care and mainte-nance. Since you are taking on the whole process rather than merely operating a funnel into the sewerage system, a greater level of care is required. Cleanliness of the pedestal and its surroundings is obviously vital, especially in a public context, the more so since dry toilets are unfamiliar and likely to be viewed with suspicion. Special attention should be paid to chutes: the longer 'skidmarks' are left, the harder they are to get off! Supplies of toilet paper and soap for washing are as normal. For public toilets paper towels are good and there should be a notice asking users to put them into the toilet chamber. If users are expected to add soak, the supplies must be maintained in the toilet room and more bought or ordered for stock if necessary. Otherwise the addition of soak should be part of routine maintenance. Peak knocking is best done regularly even if it does not appear to be necessary. Most biological systems like to have their backs scratched from time to time. The main signs of

malfunction are usually smells or flies and if these symptoms appear it is worth checking
- the vent, which might need cleaning
- the fan
- the drain, which might be blocked
- accumulations of stale urine.

This last category is usually caused by inaccurate or careless males and can be improved by appropriate notices, optional urinals and sometimes redesign of the pedestal details. Removing composted material is a roughly annual event, usually done by shovelling into sacks or wheelbarrows. Leave some in as a starter in batch systems. This might go along with a switch of seat to another position, and is an occasion to check for other problems.

SUMMARY OF BIOLOGICAL TOILET SYSTEMS
If you are new to the world of dry toilets you will probably be surprised at their complexities. This is partly because we are in a period of exploration and rapid development. As time goes on, having sorted the wheat from the chaff, we will probably end up with two or three basic designs for each level of sophistication: DIY, low-cost commercial and Rolls Royce. Size will continue to be the major issue: broadly, the bigger the better. But they all need proper maintenance. These are living systems and must be treated as such. You've got to love them.

Chapter Five
Alternative Toilets – Case Studies

This chapter looks at 'real' toilet systems and what users think of them. It first looks at toilets which, in principle, can fit into a small room and 'replace' a conventional WC. It then looks at larger composting or separating toilet systems for which building re-design might be a factor. It also considers the role of the user, small details that can make a big difference and why big is often beautiful!

Case Study No. 1 The Septum Kompakt

Fig 5.1

An unvented bucket toilet
This is a camping style urine separating toilet, with a removable plastic bag liner. The model is the Norwegian/Swedish Septum *Kompakt*. It is installed in a well-ventilated, unheated outhouse from which a flush toilet has been removed. A false floor has been fitted to accommodate the urine collection tank. (Figure 5.1) The body of the toilet is of white plastic with a hinged seat and lid. A urine-separating bowl is fixed at the front of the unit, and a plastic sack

Fig. 5.1 Location of toilet unit in an outhouse. Notice the false floor providing space for the urine-collection tank. There is also a tub for soak material and a pee-can for 'quick male wees'.

Fig 5.2a

Fig. 5.2a The unit ready for use. In this illustration the plastic sack has been lined with a three-ply paper vegetable sack trimmed to fit. There is often condensaton on the seat and regular users get into the habit ot giving a quick wipe with toilet tissue.

collects solids at the back, held in position by metal holders (Figure 5.2b).

The unit has been in use for three years, mostly by one member of the family (one of the authors) determined to give it the benefit of the doubt, plus visiting enthusiasts. Other members of the family have pointedly ignored it in favour of the inside toilet.

The sack is initially charged with soak material (see Chapter Four) and soak is added after each use. Soaks used have included sawdust, hemp chaff, earth, and RPMS (see Chapter Nine). All are adequate, but RPMS is particularly effective. There is no provision for 'peak-knocking', so the sack tends to fill rather inefficiently. Normally, emptying is required after 5-10 uses. It is occasionally slightly smelly, but not offensively so.

The unit is considered adequate for camping standards and enthusiasts, particularly males. Most of its drawbacks came from trying to separate urine and faeces. A difficulty with most urine-separation systems is the variation in anatomy between different people and the different ways people sit on toilet seats (see Chapter Six for more detail). In this case women users in particular have found it awkward and embarrassing, with many failures to achieve clear separation of urine and faeces. With perseverance, users learn how to use the toilet effectively but a single bad experience makes them reluctant to persevere. The main problem is the arrangement of the plastic sack, which should lap over the back of the urine bowl to prevent stray urine running into the main body of the unit. A useful modification is a 100mm length of plastic clip of the kind used to bind small documents (Figure 5.2b). This does not guarantee perfect separation but improves things a great deal.

Another minor design fault with this model is that the holes in the urine trap are too small and urine takes a long time to drain away. This is solved by drilling them out to 2mm. Standing urination is almost impossible without splashing and is not recommended by the manufacturers or by the owner, who has installed a pee can in the outhouse for 'quick male wees'. In this case the false floor brings the pee can to a good level for adult males to urinate without splashing or losses.

A variation not recommended by the manufacturer is replacing the plastic sack with a three-ply paper vegetable-sack. With perfect urine separation and soak material this should retain its strength and have the advantage that it does not need emptying, merely sealing and placing whole in the *ex-situ* compost container (in this installation a tyre stack, see Figure 4.10). In practice it can easily become wet and needs a plastic sack as a fail-safe container. The plastic sack would in principle be re-usable but in practice is often soiled and must be rejected. In view of this there is little point in using a paper sack as well, especially as this reduces the effective volume and needs more frequent emptying.

The unit cost £160. Flat cans suitable for collecting urine under a low floor can be obtained from camping suppliers.

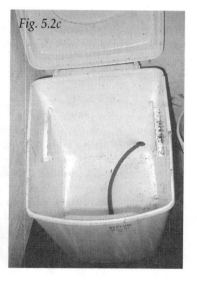

Fig. 5.2b Raising the seat shows the urine bowl. Notice the plastic binder clip securing the sack to the urine bowl. This ensures that stray urine goes into the sack and not into the body of the unit.

Fig. 5.2c With urine bowl and sack removed, the urine pipe can be seen running out through the back of the unit. The sack grips can be seen at the sides.

Case Study No. 2. The Biolet *NE*

A more sophisticated vented bucket toilet

The Biolet *NE* (Figure 5.3a&b) is a bucket toilet with several improvements on the Septum: a vent, a peak-knocking mechanism, shutters and two rigid removable containers. It is still compact enough to fit into a small room. The principle is that a newly-filled container is not emptied directly but pushed to the rear of the unit, displacing an identical container which has been in place long enough for composting to have taken place, or at least for it to have become lighter and less offensive. This 'old' container is then emptied and replaced at the front. There is a pair of shutters opened by pressure on the toilet seat to hide the contents. A peak-knocking arm is operated manually and a spring parks it conveniently to one side. The vent is not powered but is quite sophisticated, a flexible tube leading to a specially-designed insulated chimney supplied with the unit. Excess liquid drains from the bottom of the removable containers into the plastic body of the unit and out through a pipe in the base. There are ventilation holes in the base to encourage evaporation. The retail cost is about £700.

The recommended operating procedure is to start with a peat-based soak, and add more soak only once a week. The design loading is four people year-round, or somewhat more in the summer. The inactive container should remain in the unit for at least 60 days before emptying.

The trial unit was in an outbuilding at CAT, available to all staff but actually used by about 3 people in working hours. It was monitored by one of the authors, who thought:

"The toilet seemed a bit flimsy, with the moulded plastic bending slightly under the weight of a person. The flap under the seat seemed like an excellent idea as it conceals the composting chamber so you did not feel too close to the contents. However in humid conditions the mechanism became stiff and often failed to work, and finally jammed completely. The instructions that came with the toilet indicated that it would work for a family of four including the urine load. We found this not to be the case. When the toilet was used for urination the liquid did not find its way to the exit pipe as one would expect, but instead leaked onto the floor through the air vents in the base of the toilet module. This inevitably created smells and attracted flies, which deterred many otherwise sympathetic users. In other respects the sealing between lid and the chamber was good.

"The maintenance was regular and the containers were emptied roughly every two months. These were heavy and took two people to move. It was much harder than expected to push the full container along to the back, and it was easier to lift it out. Once we had struggled to get it out of the unit there was little point in replacing it and we thought it may as well go straight to

the compost heap (as we had already handled it). The material in the containers was not really composted.

"We had to impose restrictions on would-be users to keep the moisture content down, including: 'Do not use this toilet for urination only'. Prospective new users did not like the toilet as it was too complicated, smelly, and (once the shutters had jammed) a bit disconcerting to see quite how close the peak got to your bottom. We eventually decommissioned the toilet as it was unhygienic and unacceptable to have the leachate running onto the floor."

Comment:

The poor performance of this model is disappointing because unlike other models in the Biolet range it uses no electricity and held out the promise of being essentially a twin-vault system that would actually fit into a bathroom. It would doubtless work better in a heated bathroom or an outhouse in a warm climate, giving a higher rate of venting and evaporation, and more rapid composting. Two months is optimistic, although in other studies we have found good processing in the summer using RPMS and manure worms. There is a urine-separating version of this model and perhaps that would have improved things.

Probably this unit would operate well as an occasional system for summer use.

Fig. 5.3a The Biolet NE. General appearance with the lid up. The cistern-like element at the back serves as a lid stop and an attachment for the vent. The 'bomb door' shutters can be seen, which open with slight pressure on the seat.

Fig. 5.3b The top section is removable, and here the 'bomb doors' are visible from below. The two inner containers can be seen in the bottom part of the unit. A separate rigid handle is provided to lift them out and carry them away for further treatment. The peak-knocker bar is also visible.

Case Study No. 3 The Servator *Separett*

A urine-separating, powered, compact system

The Servator *Separett* (Figure 5.4a) is a compact, urine-separating toilet with a powered vent fan run either on 12 or 240 volts. Solid material collects in a removable rigid container which can be rotated by a lever after each use. This avoids the need for mechanical peak-knocking. When a container is full a lid is put on and it is removed from the unit and left for six months for further composting while a fresh container is installed. Urine is separated before it can reach the containers, and is run to a drain. There is a swinging shutter operated by seat pressure. The unit is designed for a family of four, with expected cycles of six-months between emptyings. It costs about £900. The example under test was used in an unheated bathroom by two people.

Fig 5.4a   General appearance of 12V version. (© Servator)
b) Cross section of 12V version showing essential elements.

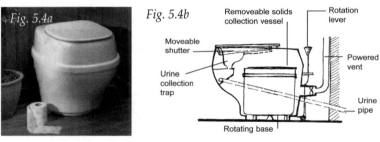

One of the users, Stokely Webster, reports:

"The hard, brittle plastic toilet module was not strong enough around the top and this led to cracking around the rotation lever, which made emptying difficult and the unit unsightly. The unit was too high even for tall people who had to lift themselves on to it with difficulty and this tended to make the hairs on the back of the legs catch on the seat – very painful. When filled to capacity, the composting chambers were very heavy. A single person using such a system would need to empty the chambers before they were full in order to be able to lift them, and hence the amount and frequency of maintenance increases. The lining of the chamber was a plastic sack which impeded the rotation of the bin.

"Flies were attracted to the smell of the toilet which was never quite alleviated by the weak extractor fan. During warm weather the composting chamber attracted flies and soon became infested with maggots. The shutter would occasionally foul outstanding deposits."

Comment:

Again this is a disappointing outcome, since we might have expected urine-separation and powered venting to produce better results than in Case Study No. 2. This kind of experience is distressingly common among users of all kinds of compact toilets, although certainly not universal. In this case it probably would have been better to use soak material and starter organisms to lighten the load and improve compost rate, and accept a more frequent emptying schedule. Although this sounds no better than a bucket toilet, the closed bins make handling more agreeable. With, say, four bins primed with appropriate organisms, effective composting could be assured.

Case Study No. 4 The Biolet *Manual*

A De-watering toilet
The Biolet *Manual* (Figure 5.5a) has all the features of an advanced de-watering toilet
• Heater with thermostat
• Vent with fan
• Emptying tray
• Integral mixer arm
• Shutters to conceal contents.
It is designed for the use of up to 4 people continuously, or more for short periods. The adjustable thermostat is turned up and down according to an excess liquid indicator tube, which operators need to keep an eye on. The mixer arm operates at two levels, one for peak-knocking and one to rake finished compost into the collection tray. In this model the arm is operated manually, with gear assist, but there is

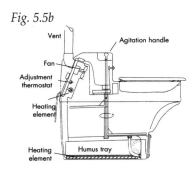

Fig. 5.5a General appearance. Here you can see the main external features – the vent, the mixing handle, the water indicator tube and the plate covering the compost tray. The shutters are the same as in Figure 5.3. The shape of the front is good: it is more comfortable to be able to tuck your legs in a bit. (© Wendage Pollution Control).

Fig. 5.5b Cross section through the unit.

an automatic version in which it is activated by an electric motor. Tray emptying is required about once a year in normal operation (see Figure 4.12) and is re-primed with a few litres of peat or similar material. The initial cost of the unit is around £1100.

Maritsa Kelly and her family lived with one of these units in a village in Cyprus. This is her report:

"We got it because water was scarce and we thought it was environmentally good to save nutrients and stop polluting water. We made a nice little room for it. Unfortunately it never worked very well and used an enormous amount of electricity - more than any of our other appliances – our neighbours used to tease us about this. Even so it never dried out, and the stuff in the tray was dreadfully wet and smelly - we had to take it a long way away into the woods. The shutters got very stiff eventually so you could see into it which was not very nice. The kids found that really disgusting, so we moved the light down so it didn't shine into the toilet. It didn't smell if the fan was running, but I got irritated by the fan going all night, so I used to switch it off.

Comment:

De-watering toilets rarely get a good press from their users and cannot really compete on level terms with a WC. In this example the family understandably tried to use it as a simple substitute for a WC in a normal home, but it could not cope. Achieving the correct level of humidity seems very difficult in spite of constant adjustments by users. In this case it would probably have been better to arrange for urine to be collected in some other way. The humid atmosphere and stray organisms (particularly the pupa-cases of flies) can play hell with shutter mechanisms and failure is common after a season or so.

Again it is somewhat surprising that such technical sophistication cannot guarantee results better than much simpler and cheaper systems. Perhaps it is a mistake to try and make toilet systems as compact as this?

Case Study No. 5 The Ekologen *DS*

A Urine-separating flush toilet

The Ekologen *DS* (Figure 5.6a&b) is a ceramic urine-separating toilet with a cistern having two operating modes: a button which when pushed allows water to flow into the toilet bowl until it is released, and a plunger which when lifted voids the complete cistern. The full flush can be adjusted between 5 and 7 litres. The toilet bowl contains an integral urine-collection section, from which a flexible pipe leads to a suitable storage, re-use or disposal system. The unit is made in small quantities in Sweden and is not readily available in the UK.

Fig. 5.6a Ekologen DS general appearance. Quite conventional. Fig. 5.6b Flush mechanisms. The central button gives a flush while it is pressed, suitable for urinations. The plunger empties the cistern. There is no float valve or siphon in the cistern, which fills quickly and quietly.

The owner (one of the authors) writes:

"This is a nice, conventional-seeming unit which looks good in the bathroom. There's the usual urine-separation problem of where to sit, little kids etc and sometimes you do get poo in the urine trap. This means you can't guarantee the sterility of the collected urine - but it doesn't happen very often. I fiddled around with the seat position a bit and now I've got it set as far back as it'll go. Standing urination is possible but the target is so small and irregular that there's a fair amount of splashing and it doesn't all go in the trap, so you lose a bit. However even a light touch on the button is adequate to remove any evidence from the bowl. This must be less than a litre. If the full flush is 6.5 litres but is only used on one occasion in four the average water per flush is just over 2 litres which is very good. The button is so easy to use one is tempted to use it even for poos and they really do disappear in the twinkling of an eye, but if one is too mean with the water the soil pipe gets blocked after a bit and needs plunging, so it's better to use the proper knob on the cistern and give poos the correct amount. On the other hand visitors often have trouble with the full-flush knob. It's hard to know how to pull it. The foul drain does tend to get blocked and it always makes a gurgling noises, so there is a need for better venting somewhere in the outlet. Just British plumbing?

"At first I thought there would be a problem with the urine trap getting blocked with toilet paper, since women usually use a small amount of paper for drying after a wee and drop it towards the front of the pan. In this toilet it does in fact land right in the urine trap every time. But in practice the lightest of flushes flips the paper neatly out of the urine section and into the main bowl, so I needn't have worried. It does work very nicely."

Fig. 5.6c

Comment:
This unit cost around £450 plus VAT to buy and more to install, then required further facilities for urine collection, storage and re-use. For more widespread takeup it would have to be cheaper and simpler to use. The urine trap seems too far back and should be set further forward. The dual-flush system is too difficult to 'read' and an arrangement such as that on the Ifö Cera would be much better (see Chapter Six).

Fig. 5.6c the pan features a urine trap at the front of the pedestal. Urine can be collected separately or run back into the main foul water drain. Compare Figure 6.8.

Case Study No.6

A Rapid-separation system with moveable container
A low-flush WC (Ifö: See Chapter Six) in a first-floor bathroom runs to an Aquatron separation unit from which solids fall into a modified but

Fig. 5.7a

otherwise standard wheelie-bin. (Figure 5.7a and Figure 4.13). Liquids are run off to a simple soakaway, the ground being suitable for this and permission granted by the relevant authorities. The wheelie-bin has a drain for surplus liquid, also running into the soakaway. The Aquatron cost £500, the wheelie-bins £100 delivered, the low-flush WC £150. Other parts

Fig. 5.7a The overall arrangement. The foul drain emerges from the wall at first floor level an runs to the Aquatron unit mounted above the wheelie-bin. For appearances' sake the structure could be fully enclosed. It would probalbly be an advantage to insulate the container.

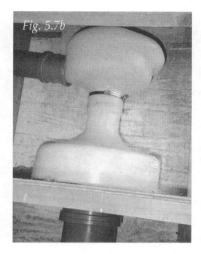

Fig. 5.7b

Fig. 5.7b The Aquatron unit. Liquids swirl around the inside surface, clinging to the walls and eventually finding their way to the outlet drain. Solids also circulate for a while, but lose their momentum as the liquids drain away, then fall down the central tube into the collection chamber.

were standard

Tom Brown, the installer and operator, comments:

"It works pretty well, although toilet paper seems to take a lot of moisture with it into the bin, which is very wet: I don't think much composting is going on in there, although I put some worms in at the beginning. I think the drain is not working very effectively – easily blocked with a combination of turds and toilet paper. It's taken 6 months to get half full, so I'll swap it soon. I could just leave the stuff to compost in the bin but that might be very slow so I expect I'll tip it out somewhere suitable. There is a bit of a problem with flies in there, and maggots wiggle their way under the lid. Perhaps they get in through the vent.

Comment:

This is an unusual but promising combination. A similar effect could have been obtained by direct drop into the wheelie bin with a urine-separating pedestal such as the Ekologen *ES* (Fig. 4.26), but the geometry of this particular site did not allow this, and a WC was preferred for use in the bathroom. The Aquatron can be used with any composting chamber of a suitable size, on a continuous or batch basis. Drainage of the container could be improved in various ways.

Case Study No. 7 Twin-Vault based on CAT design

A large, un-powered *in-situ* composter for public use.

This is not a commercial unit, but purpose-built for use by the general public in an unserviced site from a plan provided by CAT (on which Figure 4.19 is based). (See also Appendix One.) It has two passively-vented chambers each with a volume of about 1m³, one of which is active at any one time. The chambers sit on a concrete slab and excess liquid drains into the ground through a gulley. There are doors at the rear allowing access for peak-knocking and removal of composted material (Figure 4.40). The pedestal consists of a strong plastic chute with airtight seat and lid. The superstructure is of blockwork surmounted by a single-pitch roof, leaving an unglazed gap to

Fig. 5.8 Twin-vault compost toilet installed for the use of fishermen at Chard Reservoir. The pedestal can be seen through the door on the currently-active side. The abundance of trees on the site encourages a basic form of urine-separation. (© South Somerset District Council).

provide both light and ventilation (Figure 5.8). Sawdust soak is provided and users are asked to add a scoopful after each use. Brandling worms were introduced into the first chamber on commissioning. Access at the rear is via removable doors.

David Lester, Countryside Ranger at the Chard Reservoir Nature Reserve, manages the system and reports:

"The loo has been in use from 10-1-97 and so far it's worked very well, no smell or anything nasty (the worms must be doing a good job). It is mostly used by people fishing on the reservoir and they really appreciate it. I never level the contents. I recently changed the chambers over after 18 months and that was quite straightforward. I won't know what the finished stuff is like for another year."

Comment:

Although it is gratifying that our own design seems to be working so well, our experience is that unless well and regularly maintained, these simple twin-vaults in public use can become smelly and unpleasant on account of stray urine and fouled chutes. In the present case perhaps most fishermen will simply go behind a tree to urinate, only visiting the toilet for more serious purposes. As discussed in Chapter Four, this is the optimum use-pattern for *in-situ* composting.

Case Study No. 8 The M12 Clivus

A large, commercial, powered, *in-situ* composter for public use
An M12 Clivus (Figure 5.9) was installed at the Dolgoch station of the Tal-y-Llyn narrow-gauge railway in mid-Wales, for the use of the railway passengers. It is an unsupervised, unserviced location, although the unit is regularly inspected and maintained, including peak-knocking. The toilet block has two pedestals on the female side and one on the male side, plus a no-flush urinal which drains into the rear of the composting chamber. All pedestals feed through fibreglass chutes into a single chamber which has a fan powered by lead-acid batteries. These are charged by photovoltaic panels supplied as optional extras with the unit. Liquid can be drained from the bottom of the chamber through a ball valve into a collection vessel. (Figure 5.10). The system has not been in operation long enough to judge the rate of filling or the nature of the finished compost. Total cost was £7,000 + VAT plus £800 for the photovoltaic panels.

Fig. 5.9 Clivus M12 composting chamber. Notice the sloping base of the chamber, the partition to exclude fresh material (showing protruding ends of aeration baffles), the direct-drop chutes and generously- sized flexible vent tube.
(© Peak District National Park).

Fig. 5.10 The Clivus M12 at Dolgoch Falls. Here you can see it all, including the operator knocking the peak, the access hatch, the peak-knocking tool, the white aeration grille and the sump drain at the bottom. The larger tubes at the top are the toilet chutes, the angled pipe is from the urinals.

Dave Scotson and David Leach, volunteer officers of the railway, report:

"*It's only used in the summer and visitors seem quite satisfied, although there are smells and flies if the fan is not working. It's too shady for the solar panels to keep the batteries topped up so we have to swap batteries from time to time. The toilets are cleaned 3 or 4 times a week, and once a week the contents are raked and a bucket of fresh sawdust put down each chute. We use coarse sawdust and wood-shavings. In the busy season there's a fair amount of surplus liquid which we drain off through a ball-valve into juice containers and take away on the train to put into the sewer. Otherwise it can easily be disposed of to the ground: it smells a bit but isn't really unpleasant. Looks a bit like Brown Ale. Water comes from the system used to feed the trains. Used water from the sinks goes to a soakaway. The only serious complaint was from a lady who said she'd nearly lost a toddler down the chute.*"

Comment:

This is an expensive system and for this kind of money should be totally reliable. It is difficult to guarantee performance without power input to drive the fan. It would probably be an advantage to circulate the surplus liquid to the top of the compost mass to keep the wood shavings wet by pumping up through a sprinkler. For public toilets in remote locations, dry systems have the obvious advantage that they cannot be damaged by frost and will continue to be operational all year round. Water for hand washing is more problematic but is probably best addressed by collecting rainwater from the roof and storing it in an underground tank. It could be brought up to a sink by means of a foot-pump.

The public seem generally satisfied and interested. The 'toddler problem' is certainly something to think about both in domestic and public situations. Falling into the composting chamber would not be fatal but would be traumatic and seriously unhygienic. On the other hand, valuable items dropped into the toilet are not irretrievably lost.

Case Study No.9 'Euro-Dowmus'

An advanced single-chamber system in private use

This is a system custom-designed and built by Elemental Solutions in a new building, for enthusiastic householders (Figure 5.11). The flared DOWMUS toilet pedestal (see Figure 4.32) in the bathroom leads through a black plastic chute to a large composting chamber, which also receives all greywater. The tank was primed with a peat-based compost and manure worms, and softwood shavings are added regularly as soak. The tank drains to a sump, which is pumped out to a small leachfield dug along the line of a hedge. At the time of the interview it had been in use for 18 months. It cost approximately £1500. Jeremy and Claire comment as follows:

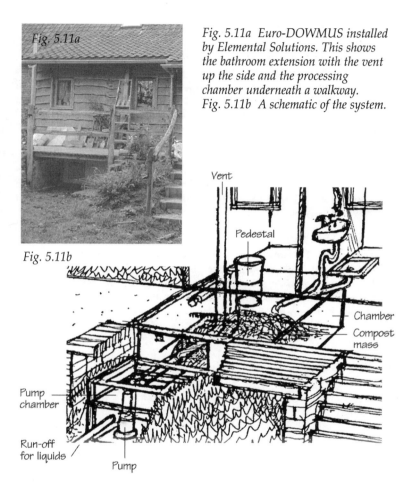

Fig. 5.11a

Fig. 5.11a Euro-DOWMUS installed by Elemental Solutions. This shows the bathroom extension with the vent up the side and the processing chamber underneath a walkway.
Fig. 5.11b A schematic of the system.

Fig. 5.11b

Vent

Pedestal

Chamber

Compost mass

Pump chamber

Run-off for liquids

Pump

"We are very happy with it, although there were a few teething problems. There were some flies at the beginning, but we never see them now. If we catch spiders in the house we put them in! When the wind was strong from the east there was a bit of a niff, but sealing the access hatch better has fixed that. Now there's never any smell at all and this is a real advantage over ordinary toilets.

"The pedestal is fine for both male and female users and for standing wees. It's even passed the grandmother test (both grandmothers!). The only people who are worried by it are some small children, perhaps because it's unfamiliar, or perhaps they are afraid of falling down the black hole! This pedestal is very wide and flanges out at the bottom so the black hole is dramatic. *We've positioned the lights so you can't see down it. The pedestal very rarely gets fouled, but if there are any marks they are easily cleaned with moist newspaper which can then be dropped down the hole. Newspaper brings up a lovely polish on sanitary porcelain.*

"*The chamber doesn't seem to need much attention: I was very surprised and pleased not to have to rake the pile much. In fact I haven't done it for 12 months. Lord knows where it all goes! The Authorities seem happy: a chap from the Environment Agency came round at the beginning and tutted a bit, but we haven't seem him since.*

Comment:

This is a situation where all the circumstances were favourable: design from the outset, plenty of space, enthusiastic and capable householders. It works in many ways better than a WC and deals with greywater as well.

CONCLUSION:

Size matters. This point seems to emerge clearly from the examples. The buffering effect of large size allows the decomposer systems to settle down, and then provides enough stability to buffer shock loads and chaotic excursions. Small systems can be made to work with luck and care, but tend to be unreliable.

Chapter Six
Water Conservation and
Low-Flush Toilets

In this chapter we look at the wider picture of water consumption in households to see where low-water and no-water toilets might fit in.

One of the main drawbacks of the WC is that it uses so much water. In Britain toilets consume a third of all household water, by far the biggest slice of the pie (Figure 6.1). This is not only water consumed, but also water seriously polluted, so in terms of its environmental impact it should rate an even bigger slice. Waterless toilets offer the prospect of cutting out this enormous slice of the pie at one stroke, and many enthusiasts have concluded that this must be the best thing to do. But here we must enter a reservation. In most existing households dry toilets do not fit easily into bathrooms, lifestyles or budgets, and can consume precious resources of money, time and management which might affect the other 60-70% of the water-consumption pie. It is often the case that more water can be saved overall with a coherent water-saving strategy and a series of cheaper, less dramatic measures than by 'going for the jugular' with a waterless toilet system.

Let's look at an example. Suppose you had £2000 to invest in water-saving measures in an ordinary house, and you found that for this sum you could buy, install and maintain a sophisticated dry toilet system that would last 25 years. Should you go for it? In

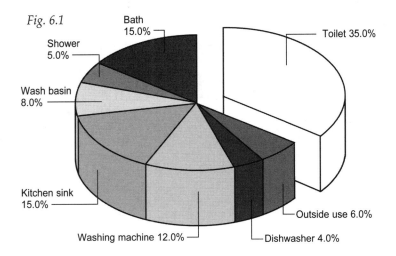

Fig. 6.1

Bath 15.0%

Shower 5.0%

Wash basin 8.0%

Kitchen sink 15.0%

Washing machine 12.0%

Toilet 35.0%

Outside use 6.0%

Dishwasher 4.0%

Fig. 6.1 Average water-consumption in British households. Household water use in Britain (and elsewhere) varies a lot from one household to another, according to differences in household size, income and lifestyles. It also varies quite a bit from one region to another. Consumption has been growing steadily for 50 years and is still rising.

(Source: Survey of Domestic Consumption – Anglian Water.)

round figures a four-person sewered household with a water meter and conventional habits and appliances might use 200,000 litres or 200m³ (cubic metres) of water a year. Installing the waterless toilet would save around 70m³ a year. Over 25 years it will have saved 1750m³. If water costs £1.50 per m³ then over 25 years the cash savings will be £2625, making a 'profit' of £625, which has cost about 57p per m³ saved.

Compare a low-flush WC with an average of 3 litres a flush, saving 40m³ a year and costing £200. In a 25-year life this saves 1000m³, worth £1500: a 'profit' of £1300 and an investment of 20p per m³ saved.

The low-flush WC does not save so much water, but is more cost-effective in terms of what-you-pay-for-what-you-get, leaving spare cash (and time) for investment in other water-saving measures such as better plumbing, efficient fittings and appliances, rainwater collection etc. In the example given we could say that while 1000m³ of savings can be achieved at 20p per m³, the extra

750m³ delivered by the dry toilet system would effectively cost £2.40 per m³, which is a poor deal because we could have used this money better elsewhere.

In a conventional setting, then, a low-flush WC would probably be the more rational choice. A dry toilet system could be more appropriate in other circumstances, particularly where the infrastructure for a WC does not already exist, for example:

• in new buildings
• where there is no sewer connection
• where there is a limited or erratic water supply
• for public toilets in remote areas.

They might also be appropriate where you can reduce costs by doing the work yourself or tolerating rather basic standards; where every other possible water-saving measure has been exhausted; or where you rate the other virtues of dry toilets higher than simple water conservation – as you might well do.

LOW-FLUSH TOILETS

Although flush toilets are generally reliable, their most common (and sometimes embarrassing) fault is that the flush does not 'clear the pan'. Early sanitary engineers were inclined to think that greater volume or greater height would solve the problem. This led to giant cast-iron Victorian cisterns requiring bell-ringer's muscles to operate. Yet when the thunderous Niagara has subsided, defiant turds are often still leering from the bowl. The 'obvious' diagnosis is wrong: the fault lies not in the cistern but in the design of the pedestal. We can now produce WC pedestals which flush solids effectively with 4 litres of water, and liquids with two litres or less, so in principle there is no need for more than this. But WC design still lags behind this standard, and the capacity of cisterns is still too great, nine litres or more being typical of older installations. Current Building Regulations set a maximum capacity of 7.5 litres per flush (soon to be 6.5) and new WC models reflect this.

Most WCs have a single flush setting, but this is not optimum because urine needs less to flush than faeces. In the past, some British manufacturers have marketed dual-flush cisterns where a short press gives a half flush, a long press a full one. These provide a good example of what can go wrong with sanitary novelties.

Fig. 6.2

Fig. 6.2 Ifö Cera low-flush WC button. Would you know what to do?

Unfamiliar users accustomed to a single-action flush could not get used to holding the button down. The result was a series of failed flushes using even more water than a single honest-to-goodness long flush, plus a certain amount of frustration and embarrassment. For this reason water authorities have discouraged the use of these dual-flush cisterns, and the new water by-laws ban them entirely – although the rules will probably be changed again to permit the best of the new types.

An ingenious recent improvement has been to reverse the pattern, with a short push for the full flush, long push for the half flush – although again this could tend to result in using more than necessary. The most recent (non-UK) improved dual flush systems either use two distinct buttons or plungers or a rocker-button (Figure 6.2)[1]. These are so unlike conventional flush levers that users are forced to think for a moment and generally get it right, especially if there is a prominent explanatory notice.

There are other low-flush systems that do not quite come into the category of dry toilets, for example the types used in temporary public toilets and on boats, trains and aeroplanes where water is scarce. The quantity of fluid required can be as little as a pint but is sometimes laced with disinfectants and other chemicals. It may be supplemented by a foam. The difficulty here is the transport of solid material, but these designs are generally not intended for use with mains sewerage but with nearby collection tanks or a direct drop into a tank below. Another alternative is a vacuum system which can draw slugs of solid material with very little water over long distances, even uphill – but at extra cost in energy and engineering complexity. These are all special cases, not likely to come into widespread household use (Figure 6.3). For public toilets in remote areas simpler but high-quality waterless systems would be usually more appropriate.

A lower limit for toilet flushing is set by the amount required to maintain the progress of solids through the pipes. Below about 3 litres there is a risk of blockages downstream of the pedestal. The most advanced continental toilets have already reached this limit. We can urge all new-buildings to specify these, and recommend them to householders who are upgrading their bathrooms.

URINALS

The main purpose of water in WCs is transport. Urine, being already liquid, is self-transporting and in theory should need no flushing at all. But in the WC it just sits there in the pan looking disagreeable. The adage 'If it's brown flush it down/ If it's yellow let it mellow'

Fig. 6.3

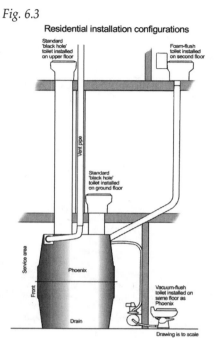

Fig. 6.3 Various low-water pedestals used in combination with a composting chamber. The Aquatron (Figure 5.7b) would be another variation here.

appears to offend modern gentility. But most visits to the toilet are in fact urinations, and this accounts for most of the water used, and wasted, in toilets. In principle, it could be far more efficient to use urinals.

In practice urinals have fallen far short of the water-saving ideal. They are usually found only in public male toilets, set to flush periodically. This flushing is usually quite independent of the pattern of use – for example, continuing during the night – and can be extremely wasteful. Timers and movement sensors (and compulsory metering of commercial premises) have improved things in recent years, but awareness is gradually spreading that in fact *urinals do not need flushing at all*. Zero-flush urinal systems have been available for at least 100 years, and there are now several different types available, some retrofits of existing urinals. Smells of stale or dried urine on the body of the urinal itself are surprisingly mild and dealt with by occasional cleaning. If urine is allowed to run smoothly off a sound sanitary porcelain surface it appears to leave very little residue. The smell of urine in the trap can be counteracted by deodorants or 'air freshener' pads of various kinds, fitted into the top of the trap (Figure 6.4). A promising new approach is the HepVo waste trap, which simply replaces an existing water-seal trap (Figure 6.5). Other systems use a layer of oil which floats on top of the urine in the trap, restricting smells (Figure 6.6, 6.7).

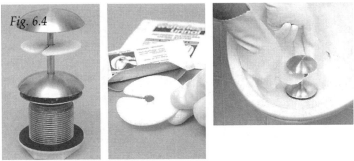

Fig. 6.4 Whiffaway waterless urinal system. A stainless steel dome is installed into the base of the urinal, beneath which air freshener pads can be fitted. The main unit is supplied free, pads cost £8.00 for six months supply.
(© Bee Environmental Ltd.)

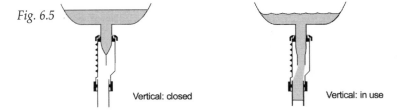

Fig. 6.5 HepVo waterless trap. The principle is simply a flattened flexible tube which is forced open by the passage of liquids but otherwise remains passively sealed. It can replace water seals in most applications and has many advantages. Its use in urinals is only just being explored. Would go well with Whiffaway system. £5.00 each. (© Hepworths Ltd.)

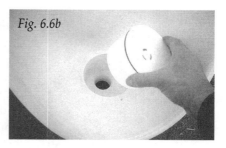

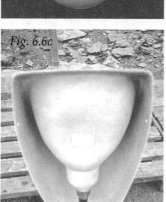

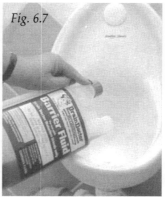

Fig. 6.7 Drain Doctor Waterless trap. Simply replaces existing trap. The trap costs £7.50+VAT, annual running cost.
(© Globemall Ltd.)

Fig. 6.6 Waterless UK urinal system with removable oil trap. There is a wide range of models, from around £250.00. Fig. 6.6a The basic unit; 6b The removable oil trap; 6c The fibreglass unit viewed from behind.

Urinals can also be fitted into household bathrooms. Of course extra plumbing provision will need to be made, and siting the unit may be difficult in some cases. Genteel householders might not like them because they tend to evoke the ambience of public lavatories. But it would make a lot of sense. There would be no need for a flushing mechanism, but perhaps a naturally-scented spray-bottle would counteract any residual smells. In certain households this alone could save 20% of water consumption, and is worth thinking more carefully about, possibly with a slight redesign of the

Fig. 6.8

Fig. 6.8 New Swedish prototype urine-separating WC. (© Nick Grant).

bathroom to tuck the urinal discreetly behind the shower unit or some other simple barrier. If the unit is too high, a step can be provided for male children to stand on. Another alternative – which already exists in many modern bathrooms – is the bidet, which operates perfectly well as a sitting urinal.

URINE-SEPARATING FLUSH TOILETS

Urine-separating toilets have a separate collecting element at the front that can lead to a separate collection tank. This is effectively a women's urinal, but also works for men sitting. The urine does not need any flush at all but a short flush (less than 1 litre) is enough to remove any paper used for drying (see Chapter Five, case study No. 5). Generally there is a clean separation of urine and faeces, although we have occasionally observed contamination of the urine bowl when the unit is used by children. Another Swedish design, by a female engineer (Figure 6.8) is probably the best so far, but they are all fearsomely expensive. The average water use per flush is around 2.5 litres for an Ekologen DS under test in Machynlleth (Figure 5.6, reviewed in Chapter Five) and near zero for an Ekologen ES in Hereford (see Figure 4.26).

CONCLUSION

From a water-saving point of view, dry toilets remain technically the 'best' solution at zero litres per visit. But we can achieve 60-80% of their water-saving potential by other means, and deliver very low overall water usage by attention to other water-using aspects of the household. In an ideal setup the use of water in flush toilets can be reduced to an average of about 3 litres per visit. This rate is compatible with a reliable WC, and maintains the porcelain standard.

Chapter Seven
Septic Tanks

Wherever there is a dwelling with no sewage connection there is usually a septic tank. One of the main choices will be whether to include it in a new system or find alternatives. This chapter aims to tell you enough about septic tanks to make this choice, and if you decide to keep the septic tank, how to make the use of it.

The septic tank is a common feature of rural life. It is a simple, reliable and effective device which is used in many 'alternative' treatment systems as well as conventional ones. For more details readers are referred to Grant and Moodie's *Septic Tanks: An Overview*[1], which is highly recommended, and to which this chapter is much indebted.

Why do we need a chapter on septic tanks in this book? Most readers contemplating alternative toilet systems will be in UNSEWERED locations. Some, probably the majority, will already have a septic tank. The reason for their interest in toilet alternatives is either that their septic tank appears to be failing, or they have been told that septic tanks are environmentally unsound. Therefore they want to explore treatment systems which do not use septic tanks. This chapter will tell them: hang on a minute, septic tanks are not so bad environmentally. If you have one, keep it; if it is not working it can usually be fixed; and fixing it is usually by far the best option environmentally as well as financially. With the information in this chapter you should be able to carry out a diagnosis and decide what to do, and you might even be able to fix a problem yourself. You will certainly learn how to treat your septic tank better.

Other readers in unsewered areas without an existing septic

tank may be intent on avoiding it, for example by installing dry toilets. But they will still be generating greywater, and this is difficult to treat without some kind of chamber bearing an uncanny resemblance to a septic tank. If they are planning one of the more flamboyant treatment systems such as reed-beds they will need to separate sewage solids and liquids, and the simplest way of doing this is via a septic tank. If you are absolutely dead set on avoiding a septic tank there are indeed ways around it, but not many!

A septic tank is entirely different from a *cesspool* which is a plain tank designed simply to store sewage until it can all be pumped out and taken elsewhere. With a typical household volume of waste-water this would need to be done every few weeks at around £100 a time – a strong if unusual incentive to use less water. Emptying would be far less frequent if there were a way of reducing the water content and concentrating the solid material. This is exactly what a septic tank does: it allows solids and liquids to separate. The liquids drain from the tank into a specially-prepared area of ground, leaving the solids to accumulate in the tank. They are pumped out and tankered to the sewage works only once a year or so. This constitutes their main running-cost and their main environmental impact.

HOW SEPTIC TANKS WORK

There are several different designs for septic tanks, but they are all closed, watertight chambers, usually with two compartments, sometimes three. The shape is quite variable – square, cylindrical, flask-shaped. Raw waste enters at one end as a mixture of solid and liquid. Some of the solids sink and form a layer of sludge at the bottom, while some – mostly fats and oils and non-biodegradable fibres – float and form a soft CRUST on the surface. This crust gets thicker over time and could block the inlet, so there is usually a T-shaped DIP PIPE which reaches both above and below the crust and can also be cleared from above if necessary (Figure 7.1a).

The liquid passes into a second chamber – usually smaller than the first – through a central port placed so it will avoid the pincer movement of the growing crust and sludge layers as long as possible. In the second chamber a similar process is repeated, but

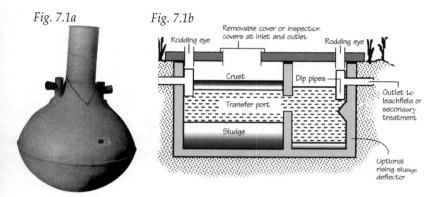

Fig. 7.1a   Fig. 7.1b

Septic Tank Designs. 7.1a Modern bottle-type septic tank,
7.1b Traditional type septic tank.

more delicately: thinner sludge and crust layers develop. Some of
the solid matter is also liquefied or suspended as very fine particles
in the liquid. Finally liquid exits the tank at about the same level it
came in, again through a dip pipe to prevent clogging. A certain
amount of gas (mostly carbon dioxide and methane) is generated
in the tank and this makes its way to the surface and out through a
vent.

The water that comes out of the tank, SEPTIC TANK EFFLUENT, still
needs a lot of treatment. The normal method is to run it into a series
of porous underground pipes called a LEACHFIELD. The water perco-
lates into the soil – a remarkably effective treatment medium – and
finally drains into the groundwater. The combination of septic tank
and leachfield serves to treat and dispose of the water effectively
and economically while retaining the option of the WC, which for
many householders is a non-negotiable element. However leachfields have their limitations and in some situations do not work at
all. Alternatives to the leachfield are discussed in more detail in
Sewage Solutions.

SEPTIC FOLKLORE

Septic tanks generate their own mythology. Stories are told of
tanks that have never been emptied and 'miraculously' treat huge
volumes of sewage. The explanation for this is usually that they are

broken. Liquids are leaking away and solids are being consumed by rats and other wild creatures, many of whom regard human excrement as a kind of *foie gras*. Properly functioning septic tanks efficiently separate solids from liquids, and water-soluble from fatty materials, but it's mostly physics rather than chemistry or biology. Of the organic material they receive, a third to a half is retained in semi-solid form, the rest emerging as liquid.

Another common tale one hears is of newly-arrived house-holders lifting the inspection hatch and, observing that the tank is 'full', rush off to phone the sewage tanker. They are confusing it with a cesspool. Of *course* the tank looks full. It always has the same surface level, determined by the position of the outlet. It is not the quantity of *liquid* in the tank that matters, but the quantity of solid or semi-solid which, if allowed to accumulate too long, will lead to blockages. On inheriting a septic tank, it is best to have it completely pumped out. Then inspect it for blockages or broken dip-pipes, have repairs made if necessary, and finally arrange for emptying on a regular basis. Once a year at a certain time is good because it helps you to remember, 'Ah, yes, the tank-emptying season is upon us.'

BLOCKAGES

Blockages are the most common problem with septic tanks. They lead to backups in the tank itself, in INSPECTION CHAMBERS on the way to it, or (oh no!) back in the toilet. A simple blocked SOIL PIPE results in flush water filling up the toilet bowl, and this can usually be cured with an ordinary sink plunger in the WC pan. If there is a partial blockage in the tank the first sign is often a dramatic gurgling sound from the WC after a flush. This is because there is a continuous body of water in the waste pipe forming a siphon. The first thing to try is (again) an ordinary plunger in the toilet. If this fails the next thing to check is a blockage to the septic tank inlet, which can be cleared by poking a stick or drain rod down the dip pipe. In most older septic tanks the inlet dip pipe will be just below the inspection hatch, so all you need to do is lift the hatch and poke a stick or drain-rod down the dip pipe. In some cases the dip pipe is accessed by a RODDING EYE in the top of the tank which is simply a hole or a tube, generally with a protective cap. In old septic tanks the rodding eye may have got covered with soil or weeds so you might have to do a bit of archaeology to find it. There will be another rodding eye at the outlet as well, and this is the first thing to try if the outlet is blocked and the tank itself is overflowing. Once you have discovered the position of your rodding eyes, keep them marked! (See Figure 7.1b.)

The most likely cause of the blockages is simply that the tank needs emptying. If after emptying the tank still does not drain properly the leachfield has itself become blocked. This might be a simple physical blockage and the first thing to try is to get it jetted clear with a high-pressure hose (the tanker contractor will advise). If this does not work there is no quick remedy. You must give it a rest for at least a year. You now have a problem of what to do with your waste water in the meantime, and you need to compare the costs and difficulties of the various options.

• The simplest remedy would be to construct another leach-field, parallel to the original. But it could be that your old leachfield has failed because it was the wrong choice or poorly designed in the first place. So first you must check the soil porosity to make sure that leachfields will work in principle on your site (see *Septic Tanks*). If the soil porosity and other indications are OK the new leachfield need not be as large as the first. The outflow from the septic tank will now run into a small chamber which allows you to divert the flow from one leachfield to the other. You will run it on the new one for a year or so, then switch back to the old one. Thereafter the two fields alternate on a yearly basis (Figure 7.2.).

Fig. 7.2

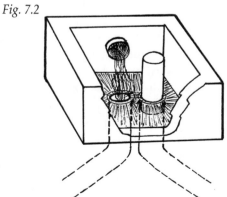

• You could install an alternative to the leach-field, as described in *Sewage Solutions.*

While the new solu-tion is being constructed you could use your septic tank as a cesspool, having it emptied every week or

Fig. 7.2 Simple distribution chamber for alternating leach field.

so: but hurry up because this is going to be very expensive! You could reduce the frequency of emptying by radical water-saving measures, including, perhaps, a temporary dry toilet.

GENERAL MAINTENANCE

One important thing to know about septic tanks is that they work best with minimum amounts of water. It does not help to 'dilute' the sewage with lots of clean water. This merely stirs up the sludge and forces foul water through the system before it has had a chance to settle out properly, and may lead to premature clogging of the leachfield. Therefore the water-conservation measures described in Chapter Six are an integral part of getting the best out of your septic tank. Using a dry toilet will reduce the quantity of water going into the tank as well as the biological load, with the net effect that the tank will need less frequent emptying and the risk of leachfield clogging is greatly reduced.

Normal detergents and cleaners will not affect the functioning of the septic tank, but mineral oils and solvents like white spirit should not be put into any waste water system.

Regular desludging of the tank is important. Don't wait for problems to prompt you!

RECLAIMING NUTRIENTS: Liquids

Septic tanks and leachfields are not designed for nutrient recovery. Leachfield pipes are deliberately buried deep so there is no interaction with the surface. Research in Australia and the USA has shown that leachfield treatment often causes nitrate and phosphorus pollution of ground water, and it is increasingly recommended that the pipes be placed closer to the surface to allow plants to remove – and benefit from – some of the excess, and for some nitrogenous compounds to be lost into the atmosphere (this is known as the 'KISS' approach: Keep Infiltration Systems Shallow).

It is commonly observed that lush beds of nettles grow above leachfields, but the rate of nutrient removal has not been measured. As far as we know, nobody in the UK has tested the simple arrangement of placing the leachfield drains shallowly (say 20cm down) in normal soil and deliberately planting species that will most effectively convert surplus nutrients into biomass. Comfrey, a robust, deep-rooted and nitrogen-hungry perennial is an obvious candidate. In the winter when the plants are inactive there will be very little uptake, so a system of this kind is most appropriate where the quantity of effluent peaks in summer – such as holiday homes and tourist facilities.

One anxiety is that the roots of such plants will invade the drainage pipes and clog them, but this has not yet been investigated. The trench arch system (see Chapter Eight) might well be the solution.

RECLAIMING NUTRIENTS FROM SEPTIC TANKS: Solids
Septic tanks are not designed for recovery of the solid material, and in the case of bottle-type tanks such recovery is out of the question. With older blockwork tanks it is possible with some ingenuity to remove a certain amount of the floating 'crust' through the inspection hatch. This can extend the length of time between emptyings and also provide some very rich material for compost making. With many tanks removing the material is tricky on account of the geometry. An ordinary shovel can only be inserted and withdrawn through the hatch more or less vertically, and crust material will tend to fall off. It has the consistency of porridge but is not so sticky. Some shovels are partially cranked and these are better. Ideally a more strongly cranked tool is needed, more like a rake with longer tines (see Figure 5.10), or an L-shaped shovel, and these need to be specially made (Figure 7.3). Once you have something of the kind it should be regarded as a precious family heirloom and passed down the generations or considered a common resource among the local community of enthusiasts. You will also need to equip yourself with a pair of long latex gauntlets and waterproof leggings.

If you are making your own tank – for treating greywater for example – you should design it with a removable lid for easier removal of the crust (Figure 7.3.).

The crust is removed a scoopful at a time and transferred in one movement to a prepared bunker or container adjacent to the tank, or to a watertight wheelbarrow for transfer to a container further away. For good composting the crust needs to be combined with

Fig. 7.3 Small septic tank with easily-removed crust. The tank is only 1m wide and covered with loose sleepers.
Removing these makes the crust accessible with conventional tools, although a cranked scoop such as that in the picture is better.

Fig. 7.4a

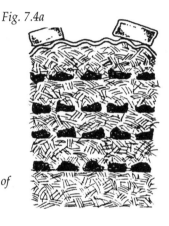

Composting septic crust. Fig. 7.4 'Rock Cakes' of crust on a bed of straw, ready for composting, 7.4a Cross section of finished heap.

some fibrous material like straw or dried bracken. 30cm or so of this material is placed in the bottom of the container and dollops of crust placed on top of it in the manner of rock-cake mixture on a baking tray (Figure 7.4). Then another 30cm layer of straw (etc) is added, then more dollops and so on. Finally the container is covered and the compost should be ready within 6 months. Turning at some point will speed up the process, but is not essential.

The finished material should be used in the same way as compost from dry toilets. (See Chapter Eight.)

CONCLUSION
Septic tanks are not as black as they are sometimes painted, and can form a useful part of a local sewage treatment system.

Chapter Eight
Greywater

Every household produces waste water. If faeces are diverted by dry toilet systems what remains is a more lightly polluted waste stream known as greywater, which has its own distinctive qualities. This chapter aims to help you deal effectively with what can be either a resource or a headache and often both.

Water from flush toilets, known as BLACKWATER, is heavily polluted with pathogenic wastes. It needs a high level of care and treatment. Waste water from other household sources – from the bath, shower, sinks, washing machine, dishwasher etc – is usually less seriously polluted and is called GREYWATER. In most houses this distinction does not matter because all waste water goes into the sewer or the septic tank and is all effectively blackwater. But for those interested in toilet alternatives and water or nutrient conservation the difference can be important for reasons such as these:

• All houses – even if they have no WCs – generate greywater, and must have a system for dealing with it.

• Households with no WCs avoid the generation of blackwater, and only need to deal with greywater.

• Some alternative toilet systems described in this book produce a liquid effluent which is essentially of greywater quality.

• Even if there are WCs, in many cases some greywater can easily be collected separately if wanted for other uses.

• Using grey water for some purposes (such as irrigation) can reduce the demand for clean water, which is one of the objects of the exercise – but you need to know how to do it .

• Greywater does contain nutrients and is potentially useful in its own right as a fertiliser.

- There are commercial systems for cleaning greywater for use in toilet flushing.
- Greywater treatment has its own particular problems to which attention should be drawn.
- We would like to encourage more experimentation to build up sources of reliable information on its treatment and use.

THE PARTICULAR PROBLEMS OF GREYWATER

Although greywater *seems* much cleaner than blackwater, it has its own erratic qualities and problems. These need to be understood if it is to be successfully treated on site, and even more so if it is to be re-used. We shall look at the various potential problems and their possible solutions.

Irregular flows and quality

Greywater comes from various sources, all different in quantity, quality and pattern of flow (think kitchen, bath, hand-basins, washing machine, dishwasher). Much of the time it's just dribbles, but sometimes a flood. Sometimes it's almost clean, sometimes it's really thick. Sometimes it's full of organic matter, sometimes detergent, sometimes grit. Sometimes it's hot.

Possible solutions:
- Surge/Mixing tank (see below).
- Only use appropriate sources on appropriate occasions.

Health hazards

Greywater from baths and showers, and sometimes washing machines does contain pathogenic organisms, which can multiply rapidly if the water is stored more than 24 hours, especially in warm conditions. .

Possible solutions:
- Do not store, use or treat quickly.
- If stored, it must be in a well-sealed tank.
- Sterilise with chemicals.

Odours

Greywater usually does not smell bad when first generated, but if stored for more than a day or so can get very smelly.

Possible solutions:
- Do not store, use or treat quickly.
- If stored, keep only in a well-sealed tank.

• Sterilise with chemicals or treat with microbial preparations.
Grease
Most of this comes from the kitchen, and when it runs down the drain it is usually warm and in fine particles. As it cools down it solidifies and sticks to things and joins up with other bits of grease, making impervious mats. Mats of grease can resist breakdown by the normal micro-organisms present in dirty water and can clog treatment systems. In a sealed tank cooled fats and oils will float to the surface given enough time, but the tank needs to be large enough for the water to cool and give the fats time to float out. Grease is one of the most difficult problems to overcome in greywater treatment and re-use.
    Possible solutions:
    • Avoid kitchen water.
    • Allow to separate in a large tank or grease trap.
    • Use while grease is still in suspension.
Solid particles
These include food wastes from the kitchen sink and dishwashers, lint from washing machines, hair from baths and showers, and grit from several sources. They can clog pipes, pumps and treatment systems.
    Possible solutions:
    • Pass through STRAW TRAP (see box 8.1).
    • Allow to settle in a large tank.
    • Use while particles are still in suspension.

Box 8.1
_____

The Straw Trap

Whatever your situation, there is one simple thing you can do to reduce pollution and reclaim nutrients and that is the straw trap, a basket of straw or dry grass inserted into the kitchen drain. This filters out coffee grounds, food particles and other bits and pieces and reduces the risk of blocked drains. From time to time (say, once a fortnight) the basket is removed and its contents dumped in the compost. Then it is given fresh straw and replaced. (See Figure 8.1.)
_____

Fig. 8.1a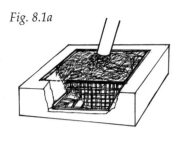

Fig. 8.1b

Fig. 8.1a Straw Filter, 8.1b An actual example. The totem blocks are not essential.

Unfavourable levels & pumps

Typically the lowest level at which greywater leaves the house is the ground – the kitchen sink and washing machine or dishwasher. Therefore any receiving tank or treatment system has to be lower than this, or it must be pumped (see box 8.2).

Box 8.2.

Pumps

Usually the pump is a submersible in a tank below ground level, operated by a float switch. One thing about pumps is that they do give you a lot of flexibility and control. They are especially useful for those treatment systems that like their dirty water to arrive in purposeful gushes rather than unpredictable dribbles and floods. It's true they use electricity, but it's not a lot – and with mains power they will probably cost you less than £1 a year to run.

The pump could get fouled with excessive grease, solid particles or hair. As so often in this field reports vary from: 'It's a nightmare, the pump is bound to get fouled up unless you really treat the water thoroughly first,' to: 'We never get any problems - no need for any fuss, just pump the stuff.'

The jury is still out.

A general pattern emerges from this list of greywater qualities and problems: that it's very hard to re-use *all* of it without some kind of treatment or conditioning. Many treatments involve a multi-purpose tank which is simultaneously a surge tank, grease trap, de-gritter, secure containment for pathogens and smelly water, and is designed to receive water by gravity and could serve as a pump chamber. *This is essentially a small septic tank.* Dealing with the effluent is dealt with in Chapter Seven and in greater detail in *Septic Tanks*.

So greywater has turned out to be much trickier than its name implies, often more problematic even than blackwater. Some people have managed to make cheap-and-cheerful systems work with very little effort. Others, for no reason yet obvious, have had endless trouble and been forced to abandon the exercise, or bolt on ever more costly and ridiculous modifications. The general conclusion for most practitioners is: *Simple disposal is better than complicated re-use*.

It is still early days in the development of 'alternative' greywater treatment and re-use. Of course we can achieve almost perfect recycling with large inputs of time, money, equipment and maintenance, but the resource is simply not worth that kind of investment. We are fairly sure that eventually we shall find simple, cheap re-use systems that will be reliable and environmentally friendly – but we don't know yet what they are.

Let us now summarise our recommendations for most house-holders with alternative toilets, as opposed to enthusiasts determined to recycle their greywater come what may:

• If you have a dry toilet but are still connected to the sewerage system, there is no pressing need to deal with greywater on-site, so you might as well dispatch it to the sewer

• If you have a dry toilet and a functioning septic tank and leachfield, continue to use it for greywater. It will probably need DESLUDGING much less frequently - only every ten years or so. Use a straw-trap, and keep an eye on the fatty crust which might be almost as thick as with mixed sewage. Consider removing some of this by hand, say every two years, to keep the tank free of blockages and the tanker at bay (see Chapter Seven)

• If you have *any* kind of working system for dealing with grey water, even if it simply runs into a big hole in the ground, stick with it

• If there is no greywater system at all, your soil might be suitable for a simple SOAKAWAY or DRYWELL. This is simply a pit, usually filled with coarse gravel, offering a big area of soil through which water can drain away. Biological activity can keep the soil from getting clogged, but only if the loading rate is not too high.

It's the simplest method (but compare the TRENCH ARCH, below), and you could do it yourself, you might even get official approval

• If official approval (Building Control, Environmental Health, Environment Agency) is not forthcoming, the most reliable, proven and legal option is a septic tank and leachfield (see Chapter Seven). If this is exactly what you were trying to avoid, a smaller tank (see Figure 7.3) would be sufficient.

TREATMENT OR DIRECT USE WITH NO TANK

What happens if there is no tank? Generally the pipes, pumps or treatment system get clogged up or are defeated by the unpredictability of the effluent. On the other hand there are many advantages to direct treatment without any intermediate storage if it could be made to work. Here are some possibilities (all improved by the elementary straw-trap described in Figure 8.1).

• **Long-established soakaway**

If your house is miles from anywhere and the greywater has always disappeared into the ground somewhere without any trouble, and the Environment Agency seems unconcerned, stick with it.

• **Hand distribution**

If you are *really* prepared to distribute all your greywater into the garden as it arises with buckets or with a hose, all year round, this will work without clogging. Nobody is really likely to do this, but see the discussion of irrigation below.

• **Willow Bank**

This is essentially a pile of bark peelings or wood shavings at least 1.5 metres deep, preferably more, with an area of 5-10 square metres, retained in some kind of retaining frame, usually a 'living structure' woven out of willows. Collected grey water runs into the middle of the pile. Solid matter is filtered out and humifies, while the liquid passes down through, promoting breakdown of the wood shavings into a compost which is an effective water-cleaning agent. Water and leached nutrients emerging from the bottom serve to feed the willows and other surrounding trees, whose roots will seek out the nutrient plume under the heap. The wood shavings need topping up or renewing every few years, and the willows need cutting back yearly (Figure 8.2).

In a small garden situation an equivalent could be a large pile of woody waste - tree prunings, hedge trimmings etc. This has not been tested but would be worth trying.

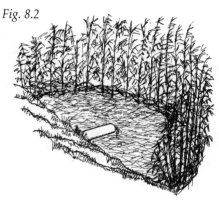

Fig. 8.2

Fig. 8.2 Willow Bank.

• **Vertical Flow Reedbed**
This is a deep, free-draining gravel-filled tank with reeds growing in it. Water flows in at the top and comes out the bottom a few minutes later, oxygenated and much the cleaner for its experience. Solids are strained out on the surface and quickly humify. It only works if the levels on the site are suitable or if the effluent is pumped. A household might have a pair of these a few square metres in area. More details are given in *Sewage Solutions*.

• **Trench arch**
This is a novel and promising idea, like an elongated soakaway. It is a long, gravel-lined trench capped with paving stones that can be pulled up for inspection or maintenance, or a row of pipes cut longitudinally in half. Raw greywater can rush along it until it finds somewhere nice to settle into. Worms and micro-organisms deal with solid matter and soon create a nice composty medium which treats the water very well. Preliminary research indicates this might also be effective for raw whole sewage, which could render this entire book redundant, so keep an eye out for this one! (Figure 8.3)[1].

IRRIGATION WITH GREYWATER
Once you do have some kind of treatment or disposal system the way is open to select certain greywater flows for use in the garden. There exist commercial greywater recycling systems which produce enough water at the right quality to use for toilet flushing and washing machines, but so far they can only handle bathroom water and are expensive[2]. If their purpose is to reduce demand for mains water it is usually far cheaper to spend the money on other

Fig. 8.3

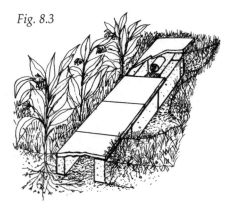

Fig. 8.3 Trench Arch

water-saving measures, as described in Chapter Six, or collect rainwater.

The ideal use for greywater is undoubtedly garden irrigation because,

• in the right circumstances it can be done very simply, usually without any pumps or filters

• the dirtiness of the water becomes a benefit because it provides nutrients to plants

• the water is cleaned in the process, although usually it cannot be reclaimed for further use.

Having said this there is remarkably little active research and experience on greywater irrigation in Britain, so we have little hard information to draw on. We have to rely on reports from abroad, notably the excellent *Create an Oasis with Greywater* by Art Ludwig, based on many years of practical experience. If you are contemplating any greywater applications, read this first [3].

Let's look at the simplest possible systems. At the very bottom is physically taking the washing-up bowl out into the garden and decanting onto suitable plants. This is an excellent system because you can target particular areas and deliver appropriate doses. On the other hand you are likely to spill a fair amount down your legs on the way, and bowls are not designed for pouring. A better way would be to pour the bowl into a watering can via a large funnel and then irrigate with the can – without its rose, which would get clogged. *Pour onto the soil, not the plants.*

The attractive feature of this 'system' is that it is so controlled. You only do it when you want or need to, otherwise the normal drainage system deals with it. You can target the water exactly where it is needed. On the other hand it does require some care and time, and will only collect say 20 litres per day, and only if you actually use a washing-up bowl in the sink.

Beyond this basic level we have to make a jump in technical

complexity and user care. You will have to go outside and see where the water comes out from the kitchen. Look under the sink and you will see a P-trap that keeps water in it all the time to isolate the sink from the outside drains. Then the pipe will either go straight out through the wall or snake along the wall a bit before going through. Generally it will emerge in a $1^1/_4$" or $1^1/_2$" (there is no metric equivalent at present) wastepipe. On the ground floor it will go into an open drain with a grille in it. This drain may also share the pipes from other waste water sources such as the washing machine or upstairs sinks, bath etc. At higher levels it will probably go into a HOPPER and come down a 3" pipe into the drain.

Consider the kitchen sink water as it comes out of the wall. You can only collect it if it emerges at a high enough level to drain into a watering can or other vessel. This requires cutting the existing pipe and inserting a hose spigot, or something similar, along with a flexible hose that can go into the can. Now what do you actually do? You have to get the empty can ready. The can is sitting there ready to receive, and you tip the bowl into the sink, or just pull the plug. The water rushes down the waste pipes into the can. If you're lucky the amount drained is less than the capacity of the can, otherwise it will run all over the yard. You have to empty the can immediately, ready for the next use of the sink, and take care never to pour down more than the can can take. What do you do when the garden doesn't need watering, or you have a lot of washing up to do late at night or you just can't be bothered setting up cans and lugging them into the garden? You want a 'default' option back into the drain, and the obvious thing is to just run the hose back into the drain. Slightly more elegant would be a diversion valve normally set to default but able to divert kitchen water into a can at short notice. But you'd have to remember to reset afterwards! Another problem is that an ordinary half-inch garden hose could get clogged with food particles, so a wide-bore flexible hose would be better – say $^3/_4$".

What about bathroom water then? This is a better bet in terms of quality, and most bathrooms are at first floor level so you've got a bit of pressure. In principle you could run this water straight through a hose and out into the garden. But how, exactly? One possibility is to siphon bath water out through a window. Another is to use a diversion valve system. Since you wouldn't want to empty the water till you've finished your bath it all works out fine. However, if your main object is to save water you should be having showers instead of baths anyway!

But this system does not work for showers unless you have the shower in the bath and keep the plug in. You could tap into the waste-pipe as it comes out of the wall, but you cannot simultaneously have a shower and be in the garden watering the plants. You would need an accomplice. Now it's all getting complicated again.

This gives some idea of the level of attention and petty detail 'simple' greywater re-use can embroil you in. If you have already sorted out your greywater system because you have no sewer connection, it would be better to simply divert it from the main treatment system into the garden. This is much easier if there is a pump in the system somewhere.

If you are really determined to invest in a proper greywater system the most efficient application would be greenhouse or conservatory irrigation. Such a scheme has been tested for several years by the Dutch environmental technology organisation De Twaalf Ambachten[4]. The grease trap, surge tank, filter and pump are all situated in the floor of the conservatory and are readily accessible. The partially-conditioned water is pumped to 32mm perforated pipes just beneath the surface of a 1m deep raised bed with plants in it. The plants benefit from water, nutrients and any residual heat. The water passes down through several layers of stratified material getting cleaned *en route* in the manner of a sand filter, and drains into a fishpond, also in the conservatory, which serves as a check on its quality but also cleans the water further. From the pond any surplus can be run off for use in the garden outside. As conservatories are also good value in terms of cheap amenity space, energy, extra rainwater collection and greenhouse facilities, to feed in greywater treatment as part of the synergy is a brilliant idea and deserves to be more widely explored. (See Figure 8.4.)

Alternatively, a small *outdoor* reedbed system is an attractive solution, although relatively expensive[5].

Fig. 8.4

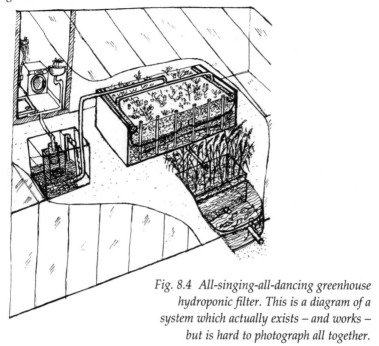

Fig. 8.4 All-singing-all-dancing greenhouse
hydroponic filter. This is a diagram of a
system which actually exists – and works –
but is hard to photograph all together.

CONCLUSION

Greywater re-use turns out to be far more complex and
problematic than we expected. Unless you are a complete fanatic,
only use it for irrigation, and then only if simple, cheap systems
work for you. If they don't, forget it. If you simply want to dispose
of it, choose the simplest method. Probably the trench-arch is best.

Chapter Nine
Nutrient Flow and Cycling

So far we have looked at toilet systems from the point of view of providing effective sanitation, avoiding · pollution and saving water. Toilets can also be looked at as part of a comprehensive waste treatment system that makes positive use of their products. This last chapter discusses the recycling and use of the valuable nutrients contained in toilet wastes.

In any toilet system the prime concern must be hygiene - treating the wastes safely and preventing the spread of disease. Second comes avoiding pollution and damage to the environment. Most of the systems described in this book fulfil these requirements. There is a third aspect: the generation of useful products, principally to improve the fertility of soils. This is often neglected but was once of much greater importance – for example in China, where a sustainable intensive agriculture system has been maintained for thousands years by meticulous recycling of all biological wastes, including human ones[1].

The most valuable constituents of toilet wastes are the mineral NUTRIENTS (see Box 9.1, compare Figure 3.2). Nutrients enter a typical household mostly in food, and divide into two streams, solid and liquid (Figure 9.1). Waste from packaging and food preparation, materials like tea leaves, coffee grounds and orange peel, and 'plate waste,' go mostly into the solid stream and exit the house with the garbage. Some goes into the liquid stream via the sink and washing up. Of the nutrients which are eaten some are absorbed into the blood stream and eventually emerge in urine, while some remain in the gut and are excreted in faeces. A very small fraction is retained for bodily growth in young members of the family, but generally speaking everything that goes in comes out in one form or another, mostly in the liquid stream as part of household sewage.

Box 9.1

What are nutrients?

By nutrients we mean elements that plants and other organisms need, apart from the 'structural' elements carbon, oxygen and hydrogen. In rough order of importance they are nitrogen, phosphorus, potassium, calcium, magnesium, sulphur, iron, sodium and chlorine, plus what are called 'trace elements', needed in small quantities but not too much, such as copper, molybdenum, boron, and zinc. Elements cannot be destroyed but they can be 'lost' to further human use – for instance in the sea, or landfills. Such 'lost' nutrients are often the cause of environmental problems.

Plants prefer their nutrients in a simple, soluble form, while other organisms usually prefer them in the form of complex organic matter which also supplies their energy. Most nutrient elements occur naturally in ordinary soils, but can become depleted or unavailable if they are removed with crops and not replenished, or if the soil organisms are inactive. In practice, long-term soil fertility is best served by adding nutrient-rich organic matter in solid form, which not only replaces lost nutrients but encourages the soil organisms to make available soluble materials for plants to take up. It also improves the structure of the soil, making for healthier plant growth.

The nutrient contents of household organic wastes vary widely, but a rough pecking-order is given in Table 9.1. Sewage-derived composts are likely to contain all necessary nutrient elements, plus energy for the decomposer organisms and are an asset to any soil. Urine is especially rich in nutrients but problematic as a direct fertiliser. It needs special treatment, as discussed in the text.

Figure 9.1 tells the rest of the story: on leaving a building, the solid stream is usually transported entire and untreated to a landfill site, where the organic waste fraction is the one that causes the greatest problems in generation of odours, potent greenhouse gases and polluting LEACHATES. The nutrients are at best wasted or at worst become pollutants. Meanwhile the liquid stream usually runs to a treatment plant where the nutrients are either discharged into natural waters[2] or incorporated into a non-hazardous but problematic material called sewage sludge. It is problematic because so much arises in relatively few places (20 million tonnes a

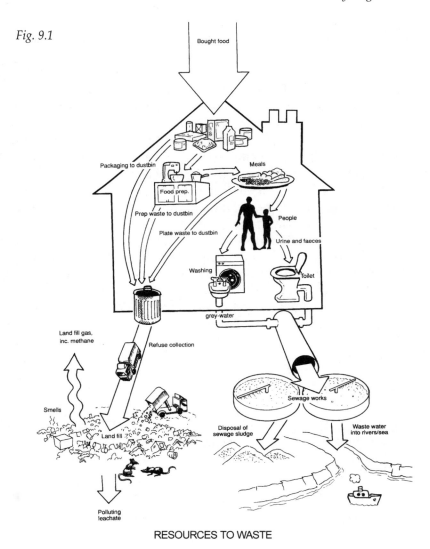

RESOURCES TO WASTE

Fig. 9.1 Linear flow of nutrients through households.

year in Britain) and a good deal of energy and transport is required to treat and dispose of it. More than half is spread on agricultural land, which can absorb the nutrients and make good use them, but unfortunately sewage sludge is nearly always contaminated with heavy metals that can build up in soils.

This is an essentially *linear* flow of resources all too character-istic of modern societies, with soil loss and nutrient depletion upstream from the household, and pollution of land, water and air downstream. An alternative, more *cyclical* flow-pattern of nutrients in a household system is represented by Figure 9.2. Material enters the household as before, but care is taken to minimise losses and to recycle nutrients as far as is practical, displacing a certain amount of bought food with on-site produce, mostly fresh vegetables and fruit which are a central part of a healthy diet.

Figure 9.2 suggests a range of practical possibilities from which ordinary householders can pick and choose - provided they have a garden of some kind. The toilet systems, urine collection and greywater are as described earlier in the book. There are three separate compost systems: a fast one for kitchen waste, grass clippings and non-recyclable paper and card[3]; a slow one for woody and other garden wastes, spent composts and urine; and a pathogenic one for dry toilet wastes if they are not fully composted *in situ* (see Chapter Four). Few people are likely to try everything here, and by way of perspective, Table 9.1 compares various organic flows.

Table 9.1

Rank	Criterion A	Criterion B	Criterion C
	Useful Nutrient Content	Ease of Collection & Processing	Safety
1	Urine	Household organic wastes	Garden wastes
2	Faeces	Garden wastes	Household organic wastes
3	Household organic wastes (plate waste, preparation waste tea/coffee grounds, vacuum cleanings, waste paper and card)	Pet litter	Urine
4	Garden wastes (grass clippings, weeds and prunings, sods)	Urine	Greywater
5	Pet litter	Faeces	Pet litter
6	Greywater	Greywater	Faeces

Fig. 9.2

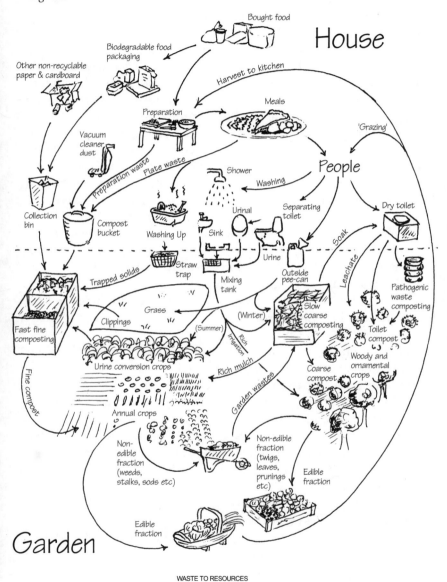

WASTE TO RESOURCES

Fig. 9.2 Ideal example of cyclical flows of nutrients in a house/garden system.

Table 9.1 ranks six common categories of household organic waste according to three different criteria, each of which has an important bearing on attempts to recycle that particular category. The ranks for Criterion A (nutrient content) apply to (say) a household of 3 people with an ordinary WC, a moderately sized garden with a small lawn, and a dog or cat – but it must be emphasised that the ranks of these categories might vary according to the size of household, size and type of garden, diet, general lifestyle etc. Garden wastes are particularly variable, from none at all to overwhelming. Common sense is needed to apply the ranks in other situations. The rankings for criteria B and C are less variable and will apply to most households, although the existence of a high-quality composting toilet will raise the faeces rank to level 2 or 3.

What does all this mean? Our view is that the six categories of wastes should be grouped into three classes according to the benefits of collecting them and retrieving their nutrients:

I: Household wastes and garden wastes.

Good yield, safe, easy, solid product: strongly recommended for any household with a garden.

II: Urine.

Moderate yield, safe, but problematic processing and use. Easier applications recommended, as discussed below.

III: Faeces, pet litter and greywater.

Moderate yield, pathogenic, problematic processing and use. Not recommended under ordinary circumstances.

Basically the conclusion is to stick to easy, tried-and-tested methods of recycling organic wastes unless you are a real enthusiast , although some simple tricks like the straw-trap (see Figure 8.1) are available to anyone. If a composting toilet system is to be installed anyway, its products can be used easily (with a few restrictions discussed below), and pet litter can be put into the chamber and processed along with the human waste. *But it is certainly not worth setting up an expensive or inconvenient dry toilet system simply for the sake of recycling what is only a small proportion of the total nutrient flow.*

However, let us assume that you are an enthusiast (like us) and you really want to try and recycle as large a proportion of nutrients as possible. We have already dealt with greywater (Chapter Eight), and the composting of faeces (Chapter Four) so now we need to look at how to use composted faeces, and urine.

A CLOSER LOOK AT HUMAN WASTES

Humans produce nutrient-rich organic matter in a wide variety of forms (see box 9.2). Although faeces and urine overwhelmingly dominate, some of the minor flows are easily and automatically recyclable. Vacuum cleaner dust is largely skin cells and does well in the compost. Hair and nail clippings, easily collected, make a good, slow-release source of nutrients for shrubs, and one of the authors has a fine shrub growing on the remains of a placenta. A certain proportion of phlegm, mucus, semen and snot can be composted routinely with soiled tissues - which should always be composted anyway. Biodegradable tampons would make menstrual blood an excellent source of iron-rich compost. Other liquid and some solid wastes will appear in the greywater flow.

Box 9.2

Nutrient streams from the members of a household

Solid	Liquid	Gaseous
faeces,	urine,	breath,
skin cells,	blood,	flatulence,
hair,	seminal fluid,	volatile organic compounds in
nail clippings,	mucus,	sweat and breath.
ear wax,	sweat,	
placentas,	tears,	
complete cadavers.	saliva,	
	pus,	
	vomit.	

Essentially these minor sources can be ignored beside urine and faeces. The quantities and proportions of these two major excretory flows vary a great deal according to age and diet. For example, the kidneys excrete surplus nitrogen in urine, and some of us have more to excrete than others: the urine of people who eat no animal foods has the appearance of lager, while that from serious carnivores is more like cream sherry, complete with a heavy, syrupy consistency. Bearing this great variability in mind, some average

statistics for urine and faeces are are presented in Table 9.2.
Some features in Table 9.2 are worth highlighting:

Table 9.2

Per adult per day	Faeces	Urine
Quantity	135-270g/day wet weight	1-1.5kg/day wet weight
	35-70g/day dry matter	50-70g/day dry matter
Water Content	66-80%	93-96%
Contents	Typical daily yield	Typical daily yield
Nitrogen	3g	8g
Phosphorus	2g	2g
Potassium	1g	2g
Calcium	2g	2g
C:N Ratio	8:1	1:2
Pathogens	100-400 billion coliforms Enterococci Streptococci	None in normal circumstances

- that even faeces are mostly water
- that although urine might seem rather insubstantial
  compared with faeces, its nutrient content is just as high, and
  for nitrogen much higher
- urine is not pathogenic under normal circumstances
- the carbon-to-nitrogen ratio of both faeces and urine is low,
  but in the case of urine dramatically so: extra carbon will be
  needed for composting.

USING HUMAN WASTES: COMPOSTED FAECES

The health question must be paramount here. No amount of
nutrient recycling can justify a tangible risk to human health.
Accordingly we have to say: don't do it unless you are really
committed to making it work safely and reliably. If you do have a
compost toilet the solid product should be pleasant, about as
pathogenic as garden soil, and immediately usable. But it is *possible*
that some pathogens could survive; that somehow the compost
process did not work properly, or mature material was somehow
contaminated with fresh. For this reason we recommend that *toilet
compost should be kept separate from other organic waste streams* and
only used where there is no chance of contaminating edible crops.

Purely ornamental parts of the garden are OK, and it could be used for woody crops – trees and bushes where the edible parts of the plant are well away from the ground, and where the plantings are permanent and there will be no low growing crops in subsequent years. Pathogens cannot enter a plant and travel into the edible parts, but they could be thrown on during cultivation, or splashed on by rain. We must emphasise that in almost any circumstances the risks are extremely small but you might as well establish 'good practice'. This is reflected in Figure 9.2, which also suggests a source of soak material for a dry toilet: coarse garden compost derived from weeds and woody waste.

That is probably all there is to say about using composted faeces: be careful, but otherwise use it like ordinary compost on appropriate crops. Urine, to which we now turn, is much more challenging.

Box 9.3

The Great Nappy Debate

Great angst is generated over nappies in the environmental movement. Should we not use washable cloth nappies? For fear of getting lynched we hesitate to venture an opinion, but what are the implications for the fate of the waste? Basically what happens is that with cloth nappies the wastes go into the liquid stream and the sewerage system, while with disposable nappies they go into the solid stream and to landfill. Neither is an ideal option. Washing nappies has an environmental cost in detergents and energy for heating water, while the active content of nappies in landfills is likely to turn partly into methane, a powerful greenhouse gas. In either case the nutrients are lost.

Can householders do anything to improve matters? Sadly rather little, except perhaps to scoop out and compost (in the pathogenic stream) the more solid productions of their young children. At CAT we have tried composting disposable nappies with almost zero success, since the potentially compostable elements are enclosed in impervious plastic membranes or meshes which decomposers cannot penetrate. The ultimate answer, we feel, is biodegradable disposables. These could be dealt with either by householders themselves, or collected separately for composting on a community or municipal scale.

USING HUMAN WASTES: Urine

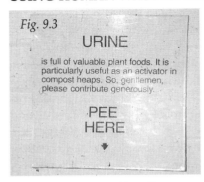

Fig. 9.3

URINE

is full of valuable plant foods. It is particularly useful as an activator in compost heaps. So, gentlemen, please contribute generously.

PEE HERE

↓

Fig. 9.3 Sign in a public toilet at C.A.T.

Urine is a rich source of nutrients, and a household generates prodigious quantities, even if, as is often the case, it is only collected from the male members (Figure 9.3). Urine plus household and garden wastes (all the non-pathogenic streams) are likely to account for over 80% of the total nutrient flow - more than is needed to fertilise even a very large garden. In institutional buildings the quantity of urine can be very large indeed, and if collected separately (see Chapter Six) can be stored, removed in bulk and used as a farm fertiliser, as is done in some parts of Sweden.

Using urine in the garden is a bit more complicated. The most obvious thing is to water it directly onto the soil in the manner of soluble commercial fertilisers. This is possible, but has some disadvantages. Firstly, urine contains a lot of sodium so is salty and in high concentrations toxic to small organisms and plant roots. Secondly, its ingredients are highly soluble in water, so can be rapidly leached out by rain and lost into the ground water. Thirdly, the nitrogen in stored urine, initially in the form of urea, quickly breaks down to ammonia, especially in warm conditions. Ammonia is volatile (lost into the air), smelly, and very poisonous to small organisms. For all these reasons it is not a good idea simply to fertilise crops routinely with neat, stored urine. So what else can we do? We are in little-known territory here, but have explored a number of possibilities, either singly or in combination:

1. diluting it
2. combining it with greywater
3. using it only under special circumstances
4. using special conversion crops to absorb its nutrients
5. incorporating it into pre-existing compost processes
6. absorbing it on suitable materials and composting the result.

This is very much work in progress, but for what it's worth we would like to end this book with what we have learned so far about recycling urine.

Diluting Urine

The effects of neat, stored urine can be observed if a watering-can-full is emptied, without a rose, haphazardly across a lawn. Within a week, a brown line develops where the grass has been 'burned'. It usually recovers later, but it is much better to dilute the urine at least 1:5, preferably 1:10. It is a good rule of thumb always to dilute urine for direct use, even if it is fresh. 1:20 is good for houseplants from time to time during the summer.

A commercial device that both collects and dilutes is the ingenious 'Ejektortank' from Sweden (Figure 9.4), designed to receive urine from urine-separating toilets. It has a capacity of about 30 litres, and a float gauge so you know when it's getting full. Then you attach an ordinary garden hose to a connector on one side of the lid and apply mains pressure. Like a paint sprayer this pulls out the urine and dilutes it 8:1, delivering it to another hose on the other side of the lid, which ends in a short lance applicator. The urine can then be distributed between crops or over a lawn. The same device could be used to distribute smaller quantities of drainage liquor from composting toilets (Figure 9.4b).

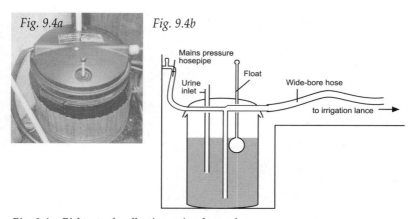

Fig. 9.4a Ejektortank collecting urine from a house
Fig. 9.4b Possible arrangement for Ejectortank.

Diluting Urine with Greywater

The downside of dilution is that the addition of extra water slightly contradicts our efforts elsewhere to save it. To avoid this, another possibility is to combine urine with greywater directly from a dwelling without any intermediary treatment. Greywater is too low in nutrients, urine too high, so in principle they are good companions. Further, both urine and greywater deteriorate if stored so it is better to use them swiftly. An experimental trial of this idea is illustrated in Figure 9.5, where bathroom flows are combined and filtered through a straw trap, then run to perforated pipes buried in mulch on the surface of the soil between crop rows. With a urine-separating toilet giving dilutions of 1:3 and the extra greywater giving variable extra dilution of up to 1:10 the soil should be able to absorb the nutrients fairly comfortably. The response of plants and soils to continual mixed dosing of this kind will be monitored over a period of several years.

Fig. 9.5a

Fig. 9.5b

Fig. 9.5 Mixed greywater and urine system in a house with urine-separating toilet. 9.5a Mixing hopper and overflow. The thinner pipe on the right comes from the urine-trap, the thicker pipes from sink, shower and bath. The 1½" drainpipe on the left runs to the header tank. An overflow is provided by jamming a short piece of 3" pipe into the downpipe. 9.5b Surge and header tank with straw trap. this gives a head of about one metre above the soil. The straw is contained in a small basket fixed to the side of the tank. There is a well-fitting lid to prevent smells.

Special circumstances for direct use of urine

There are circumstances when direct fertilisation with urine is advantageous, although research on this is at an early stage. We have observed that urine has little effect on plants growing in fertile organic soils in the summer, but a strong effect in the winter and early spring. This is probably because in warm, rich soils there is plenty of nitrogen available for the plants, but in cold soils it is hard for the plants to pick up enough, particularly if their root systems are still not fully grown. This is the reason why farmers give a 'nitrogen boost' to their crops in the spring with (for example) nitro-chalk, to wake them up and get them going. Urine does very well in this regard, and we have observed greatly increased yields of winter onions, garlic, leeks, cabbage, early carrots and lettuce. We use it diluted 20:1, applied to the surface of the soil around the plants about once a week in late winter and early spring. Figure 9.6 shows an example of the effect. This is impressive but should be regarded as a special case. As organic growers never tire of saying, soluble nutrients, no matter how 'natural', are really a kind of horticultural junk food and do not build up the underlying health of the soil. It is much better to feed the soil with solid material. How then can we convert the nutrients in urine into a solid form?

Fig. 9.6 Effect of dilute urine on yields of winter onions. There were three rows 30cms apart, urine being applied outside the right-hand row. The middle row was also influenced by the urine, but less than the right-hand row.

Conversion crops

One possibility is to grow certain specialist plants which will take up the nutrients from liquid urine and turn them into leaf. These plants can then be used as rich surface mulches, or composted. One plant which famously tolerates very high concentrations of nitrogen is COMFREY. It is a large, fast-growing plant with very deep roots. It is not killed by neat, stale urine applied in large quantities, as we have established at CAT, but we do not know what proportion of the nutrients are intercepted and taken up. Neither do we know what size of plot would be needed to 'launder' a given amount of urine. The plant clearly responds to this kind of treatment by producing huge leaves, and the leaves are well-known to be rich in protein and potash, and excellent for animal feed. It also makes excellent compost and mulch, and has many other uses, notably as a slug decoy. Slugs like wilting comfrey so you can use comfrey leaves around susceptible crops to distract them. Generally this stops working after the beginning of July owing to biochemical changes in the comfrey, but urine-fed plants remain effective for several weeks longer – an agreeable bonus.

An alternative approach is to use lawns. A lawn does not need feeding with organic matter because it constantly generates its own. But constant mowing does remove nutrients which need replenishing, and urine provides an ideal source. It should be applied diluted at least 1:10 and applied via a watering can rose (or a device such as Figure 9.4) as evenly as possible, ideally before rain else it should be followed with plain water to wash it off the leaves into the ground. This fertilisation will make the grass grow stronger and faster, and very green. It will also kill moss. You will need to mow it more frequently of course, but that is the whole point: to harvest instant mulch or readily-compostable green material. In Figure 9.2 grass mowings are shown going into the fast heap along with paper and kitchen waste. They are very clean and break down rapidly, and need the extra paper and cardboard to stop them clumping into a soggy mat.

Incorporating urine into compost

The late, great Lawrence Hills used to recommend what he coyly called 'Household Liquid Activator No.1' to gee up sluggish compost heaps. He meant of course, urine, and indeed the fresh stuff from a chamber pot, or more directly when nobody is looking, does seem to have a beneficial effect. On the other hand most compost heaps already have too much nitrogen, so adding large quantities of stored, neat urine is not helping the carbon-to-nitrogen balance and could waste a lot of nitrogen and even do some damage to the decomposers through excessive ammonia. What we need is highly carbonaceous material that will balance the very high nitrogen in the urine. In the idealised scheme shown by Figure 9.2 we show a separate coarse/slow compost system with much higher levels of fibre and carbon which takes all garden waste except grass clippings; that is weeds, leaves, twigs (perhaps shredded), prunings, soil clods, spent potting mixes and so on. It is in fact more or less what many gardeners do anyway – just have an indiscriminate dump round the back of the shed somewhere. Such a heap is apt to be short of both nitrogen and moisture – a perfect foil for urine, and it will produce beautiful compost in the fullness of time. This compost will also make a good soak for dry toilets.

A system like this is preferable to bonfires, which are a tremendous waste of precious carbon. John Beeby of Ecology Action in California in his fascinating monograph *Future Fertility*[5] analyses the acreage of crops needed simply to grow the carbon necessary to balance the nitrogen in human wastes and turn it all back into useful compost. *It is more than half the total growing area.* So we should look after our precious carbon, and combining woody wastes with urine could be an important way to do it.

Special urine-composting systems

Good composting needs carbon, nitrogen, water and air. Urine has plenty of nitrogen and water. Fibrous materials like straw have carbon and air. This is the basis of the 'straw bale urinal'. A bale of straw (not hay) with cut ends uppermost is left in a shady spot. You wee directly on it whenever convenient. For men it is fairly straighforward. Women can simply 'stand astride' the bale, or sit on two narrow planks, or indeed dangle from a branch if the bale is well-placed. The effect is to allow urine to percolate down into the bale and start the composting process off. Occasional use in this manner will provide enough nitrogen, and then the bale is just left

Fig. 9.7

Fig. 9.7 Straw-bale urinal. This one has been opened up rather prematurely but shows the humifying centre.

to the weather and its own devices. Eventually (six months to a year later) it is opened up to reveal fine blackish compost, which can be used directly (Figure 9.7). Alternatively the bale can be broken up at any time and fed into the regular compost process, or used as a loose mulch on the surface of the soil.

It is very striking that huge doses of neat, stale, stored urine have the opposite effect and pickle the straw, which then takes much *longer* to break down. Once again dilution, or freshness, seem to be important.

An 'urban' version of the straw-bale urinal is a plastic box full of corrugated cardboard with the flutes arranged vertically. Urine runs readily down the flutes, which eventually become home to an impressive variety of decomposers (see Figure 9.8.) Figure 9.9 shows a more whimsical but similar idea. Although paper and cardboard can provide an ideal source of carbon in the form of cellulose, this simple combination with urine takes a long time to get going. The reason is that the decomposer animals cannot use the nitrogen in urine, but must obtain it from complex proteins. Proteins can be provided by moulds growing on the paper, who *can* use the nitrogen in urine, but cannot really establish a foothold without the animals to rough things up, make holes and provide access into the paper. So we have a 'protein gap' which slows the process down. This can be bridged with a small amount of fresh plant matter, such as grass or comfrey leaves, which acts as a catalyst for the whole process. Somewhere in here there is the germ of a complete nutrient recycling system. Watch this space.

Fig. 9.8   The cardboard/urine bioreactor.
Fig. 9.8a   Day one.
Fig. 9.8b   After nine months.
Fig. 9.8c   After eighteen months.

Fig. 9.9

Fig. 9.9 Composting urine with paper as a carbon source. In this case urine was 'administered' from time to time to a row of unwanted books in a washing-up bowl and left for nature to take its course. This picture shows the state of breakdown after nine months. After two years the books were reduced to a perfect soil-like compost – with the exception of the plastic cover of 'The Doctor's Two Lives'.

CONCLUSION:

For any household or institution with access to land, recycling the nutrients in organic wastes can be a strong contribution to environmental quality. Toilet wastes can be problematic, but progress is being made towards treating them safely and effectively, and making good use of the riches they contain.

Appendix One
Plans for a Twin-Vault
Composting Toilet

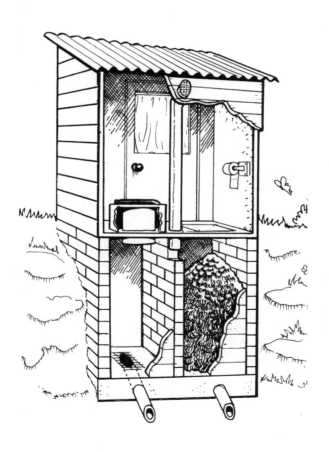

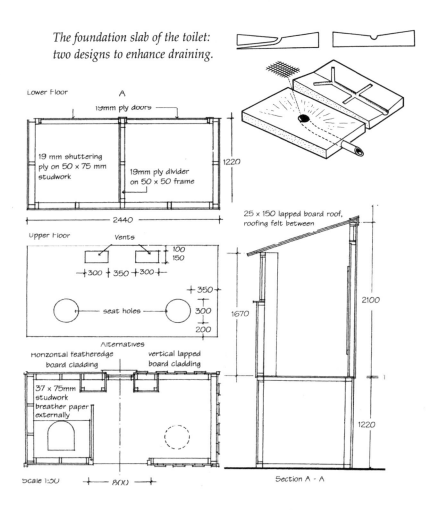

The foundation slab of the toilet: two designs to enhance draining.

Lower Floor   A

19mm ply doors

19 mm shuttering ply on 50 x 75 mm studwork

19mm ply divider on 50 x 50 frame

1220

2440

Upper Floor   Vents

100
150

+300 + 350 +300+

+350+

seat holes

300
200

1670

Alternatives

Horizontal featheredge board cladding | vertical lapped board cladding

37 x 75mm studwork breather paper externally

25 x 150 lapped board roof, roofing felt between

2100

1220

Scale 1:50   +— 800 —+

Section A - A

The general principles outlined in Chapter Four should suffice for you to design and build a twin-vault toilet system to suit your own tastes and circumstances. But for those who would prefer more detailed instructions we have created an all-timber design based on standard 8 x 4 plywood sheets.

The result is a big unit with a very generous chamber size, suitable for up to ten users. You don't have to stick literally to the dimensions, but as given they minimise the amount of cutting. The instructions are not detailed enough for absolute beginners — you need to know a bit about building techniques. After reading what follows, if you're still mystified, get some help, or do an 'Alternative Sewage' course at C.A.T.

Pour the foundation slab first, at least 10cm deep, using 5:1 sand/aggregate to cement. The shuttering can be very simple – 10cm boards nailed together to form a box, sitting directly on firm ground. The exterior dimensions of the shuttering are 8 x 4, like the floor plate, so the slab is slightly smaller than the structure. If there is a drainage tube, place it before pouring and trim later; any profiling for drainage is done by hand after pouring; it has to be done separately for each vault to ensure that there are good falls away from the woodwork.

Make up each of the plywood-and-batten panels for the vault separately, then nail, screw or bolt them together. Bolting is expensive, but useful if you have to move the structure. Cut out the seat and vent holes in the plywood floor-panel and fix this on to the base. Vault-door designs are up to you. You now have a functioning twin-vault toilet but little comfort and no privacy.

The seat is designed according to the text and your taste (see for example Figure 4.23); in this particular layout it is beside the main

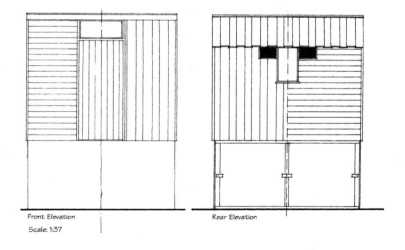

Front Elevation

Scale: 1:37

Rear Elevation

door, so make sure it does not prevent the door being opened. The superstructure is made up of studwork frames like the base, without plywood sheathing. Once erected, drill a hole between each pair of vertical studs through the bottom members, through the floor and the upper members of the base frames, and secure the superstructure with 10mm bolts (or threaded rod) through these holes. We have suggested wooden boards for cladding, and these can be arranged vertically or horizontally. The roof, like the floor, is essentially plywood covered in roofing felt and clad with lapped boards. Cladding the toilet interior is optional.

The vents are made up from studs and pieces of ply, and must be well-sealed up to the screened openings. The gap between the vents in this design suggests the possibility of a small cupboard (for cleaning materials etc.), or at least a shelf below the window for flowers.

Good luck!

Appendix Two
A New Design of Twin-Vault
Toilet from Natural Solutions

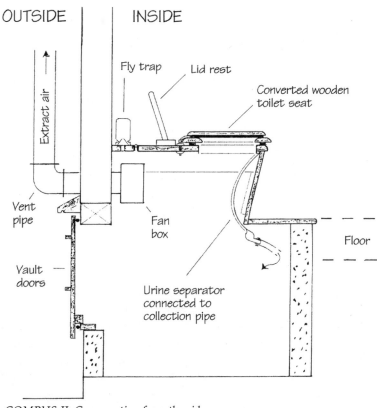

OUTSIDE   INSIDE

Extract air →

Fly trap   Lid rest

Converted wooden
toilet seat

Vent
pipe

Fan
box

Floor

Vault
doors

Urine separator
connected to
collection pipe

COMPUS II: Cross section from the side.

Plan

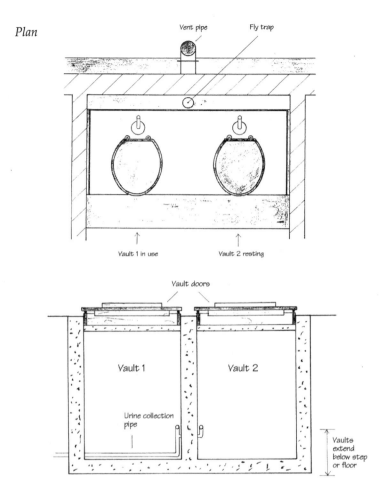

Plan section of vaults below step (or floor) level.

I built my first toilet several years ago after studying the design in *Fertile Waste*, C.A.T.'S previous publication on composting toilets (Appendix One). In the spirit of experimentation, I made radical departures from that design and it became affectionately known as 'The Aga' due to a size and appearance similar to that of a solid fuel cooker. Several years' work on this, including some further departures and some movement back towards the original *Fertile Waste* design, has produced COMPUS II, a compact, composting, urine separating, twin vault toilet.

Front view

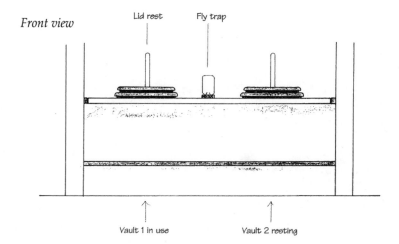

Urine separation is the most significant difference between this design and the design shown in Appendix One. Urine separation is not a new concept. It is a principle which has been employed in various lo-flush W.C.s and is found in some 'bucket toilets'. (See Chapters Five and Six.) However, it has not generally been utilised on twin vault composting toilets.

There are several advantages to urine separation:

There are no additions of soak material made after micturition (i.e. after peeing). This helps to reduce the size of vault required and the quantity of soak needed.

There is little or no production of blackwater – sometimes known as compost tea (!) – at the bottom of the vault in a urine separating toilet. Consequently no blackwater drainage is necessary. It is more likely that the contents of a urine separating composting toilet may become too dry for effective decomposition and that the addition of some water will be necessary.

The experience of a number of compost toilet users seems to confirm that most smells from composting toilets are due to urine or the combination of urine and faeces. This is because urine is high in nitrogen and allowing it into the vault makes the vault contents too nitrogen rich. Urea decomposes to ammonia and this is quite smelly stuff. Separating urine largely eliminates smells.

With the exception of one or two rare tropical diseases, urine should be non-pathogenic and contains very useful nutrients. It is

Looking through the vault door

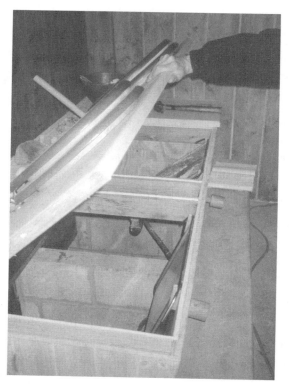

The top of the box is hinged and can be lifted for inspection. The urine-separating plate in its normal position can be seen in the near chamber with the wooden angle-adjusting screw.

Front view of COMPUS II, showing seats and footrests.

almost certainly the best fertiliser you can easily obtain and it's free. Urine separation avoids contamination of the urine from faecal material and makes collection easy. Hence it is good practice for gardeners (see Chapter Nine).

One of the problems with most urine separating systems is that they are easily fouled, usually by children sitting too far forward on the seat or by adults and children being careless when adding soak. With regard to this latter issue, I have recently come to the conclusion that soak is best added daily by a manager rather than by each user. The type of urine separator shown in outline in the cross section on page 137 and Figure 4.28 relies on surface tension to guide the urine into the collecting trough. Solids do not easily follow the curvature of the separator and should end up in the vault.

There are two other developments which are not linked to urine separation:

Fan assisted ventilation using a low wattage fan is a particularly good idea. A basic layout is shown in the cross section (page 137). Electricity consumption can cost as little as £3.00 to £4.00 per year even with the fan running continuously and the vent pipe can be narrower than with passive ventilation and is therefore less expensive to install. Passive ventilation may not work at all in adverse wind conditions or when you most need it to, i.e. when the lid is raised and you are in position on the toilet.

It seems common practice to fit chutes to dry toilets as in Appendix One. This seems to me to be an attempt to carry on the appearance and structure of a WC with little good reason. Perhaps it is just an evolutionary hangover in toilet design, like the appendix in the human body. The only logical reason I can find for retaining chutes is that they do tend to hide the vault contents from view (see Figure 4.19). The downside is that unlike the pan in a WC the chute is not regularly cleaned by flushing and soon becomes unpleasantly soiled. So, I have avoided chutes on this design even though it does increase your view of the poo.

Finally a word of thanks to the people who generously provided the raw materials for this research.

Andy Warren June, 1999.

Further details of the COMPUS II can be obtained from Natural Solutions, telephone: 01686 412653.

Notes

Introduction

1 The Centre for Alternative Technology, Machynlleth, Powys, SY20 9AZ; Tel: 01654 702400 general enquiries, 01654 703409 for mail order; email: orders@catmailorder.demon.co.uk; website: http://www.cat.org.uk

2 *Sewage Solutions: Answering the call of nature*, N. Grant, M. Moodie & C. Weedon, CAT Publications, ISBN 1 898049 13 0

3 *Septic Tanks* (see note 7.1), *Creating an Oasis* (details in text), *Safe to Drink?*, Julie Stauffer, CAT Publications, 1996. All available from the Centre for Alternative Technology mail order or bookshop

4 *The Humanure Handbook*, Joseph Jenkins, 1997.
Das Scheiss Büch, Werner Pieper (ed), Der Grüne Zweig, Lohrbach. Available from CAT by mail order (as above).
See also *Compost-Toiletten*, Claudia Lorenz-Ladener (ed), Ökobuch, Freiburg, 1992

Chapter one

1 *Risk and Culture*, Mary Douglas and Aaron Wildausky, University of California Press, 1982

2 *The Anatomy of Disgust*, William Ian Miller, Harvard University Press, 1997

Chapter two

1 See for example *Water Treatment and Sanitation: Simple Methods for Rural Areas*, H. T. Mann & D. Williamson, Intermediate Technology Publications, 1982 (available from the CAT bookshop)

Chapter three

1 *The Humanure Handbook*, Joseph Jenkins (as above)
2 See *Sewage Solutions* for discussion of legal aspects
3 See note 4, Table 4.1 page 65

Chapter four

1 In-situ/ex-situ: these curious Latin terms are the most concise way we have found to label the difference
2 *The Humanure Handbook*, Joseph Jenkins (as above)
3 DOWMUS stands for Domestic Organisations Waste Management and Use Systems and the original design is illustrated in *Sewage Solutions* (CAT Publications)
4 See for example *Water Treatment and Sanitation: Simple Methods for Rural Areas*, H. T. Mann & D. Williamson, Intermediate Technology Publications, 1982 (available from the CAT bookshop)
5 See for example *Privies Galore*, Mollie Harris, Alan Sutton Publishing, 1980, and *Thunder, Flush and Thomas Crapper: An Encyclopedia*, Adam Hart-Davis, Michael O'Mara Books, 1997

Chapter six

1 Ifö toilets and fittings can be obtained in Britain via Elemental Solutions, Oaklands Park, Newnham, Glos, GL14 1EF, tel: 01594 516063, fax: 01594 516821

Chapter seven

1 *Septic Tanks: An Overview*, Nick Grant & Mark Moodie, Elemental Solutions, 1996, available from CAT via mail order

Chapter eight

1 The trench arch idea has been developed by Elemental Solutions and is still under test.
2 Commercial systems include the Water Dynamics system (1a New Street, Mawdesley, Ormskirk, Lancs, L40 2QN) and the Aquasaver System (Unit 3, Efford Farm Business Park, Vicarage Road, Bude, Cornwall, EX23 8LT)
3 See Introduction, note 3
4 De Twaalf Ambachten, Mezenlaan 2, 5282 HB Boxtel, The Netherlands. This drawing is adapted from *Alternatives for Sewage*

Systems, a treasure-house of ideas which also covers the dry toilets mentioned in this book

5 See *Sewage Solutions* (details as above)

Chapter nine

1 See for example the classic *Farmers of Forty Centuries*, F. H. King

2 Excessive nitrogen and phosphorus from human sewage can cause severe pollution problems through their effects on aquatic plants. In coastal waters they cause algal blooms which may be toxic to people and fish, and in enclosed bodies of water such as Lake Victoria whole ports can be blocked by large plants such as water hyacinth

3 Composting household paper and card has been much investigated at CAT, see *Composting Secrets*, CAT Publications. For further details contact the Biology Department at CAT.

4 Although this slug decoy system has worked well in trials at CAT, it did not work very well for members of the Henry Doubleday Research Association who tried it. If you would like to give it a try, send for the CAT tipsheet on Slugs

5 *Future Fertility*, John Beeby.

Glossary

Ammonia – NH3, a compound very commonly released in the decomposition of organic matter, especially under anaerobic conditions, which is both smelly and in high concentrations poisonous to decomposer organisms

Aerobic conditions – allow aerobic processes to take place: open texture, not too much liquid. In composting, this usually requires some fibrous material and/or periodic 'turning' of the compost mass.

Aerobic processes – composting where oxygen is an active participant. The breakdown of organic matter is usually rapid, generates heat and does not smell offensive. Chemically it is related to burning.

Anaerobic conditions – circumstances that give rise to anaerobic processes, e.g. excessive liquid content, impervious surface layers, sticky texture.

Anaerobic processes – decay processes that occur in the absence of oxygen; 'putrefaction', usually slow and smelly.

Blackwater – water contaminated with *faeces*; or any water containing a significant proportion of pathogenic organisms. In the domestic context it usually refers to that from a standard flush toilet.

Batch Process – a discontinuous process in which all the ingredients are processed, and eventually harvested, simultaneously. Contrast 'Continuous'.

Bio-aerosols – micro-organisms suspended in the air, often in water droplets.

Brandling Worm – a small lumbricid worm *Eisenia foetida*, which has been found particularly effective in treating organic wastes. Other useful worms include *Lumbricus rubellus* and *Dendrobaena*. These are all fairly common and often found in compost heaps.

Bucket Toilet – a toilet system with moveable container to allow regular emptying. They serve only to collect material, not to process it.

Cesspool – a tank used to collect and store waste water. It has no outlet and must be emptied when full.

Chute – in this context a tube to convey human wastes from the pedestal to the processing chamber.

Comfrey – *Symphytum officinale* – a broad-leaved herb with small tubular flowers. Prefers damp areas. Leaves have a high protein content and the plant thrives on high nutrient inputs.

Composting – deliberately controlled use of the natural process by which living tissue and its by-products break down into stable soil-like material.

Continuous Process – a steady-state process in which the early and late stages of processing are present in the same unit. Contrast Batch, q.v.

True Composting toilets – toilets (usually dry) where complete treatment of sewage waste occurs *in situ* (q.v.).

Crust – material floating on top of septic tank effluent (or other body of waste-water) made up of the lighter components of sewage and greywater. Exposed to the air these slowly compost.

Decomposition – the process in which complex biological structures and molecules are broken down into simpler ones, often through the action of decomposer organisms.

Decomposer Organisms – organisms which specialise in the breakdown of organic matter. They include fungi, bacteria, and invertebrates such as worms, mites and nematodes.

Drywell – american term for a soakaway.

Desludging – process by which sewage sludge is pumped out of a septic tank or cess pool for treatment elsewhere.

Dewatering – process whereby water is removed from sewage by heat or forced draught. The sewage matter is sterilised not composted, and its volume greatly reduced.

Dip pipe – T-shaped (on its side) pipe that allows liquid from below the surface to leave a tank while retaining the surface material.

Ex-Situ – the processing of wastes remotely from the pedestal. Contrast *In-situ*. q.v.

Faecal pathogens – organisms found in faeces that are harmful to human health.

Fly trap – device fitted to a compost toilet designed to attract, trap and kill flies, keeping the toilet pedestal free from nuisance.

Greywater – non-pathogenic waste waters. In the domestic context this means all waste waters except those from the flush toilet.

Hopper – an open-topped chamber, usually mounted on an outside wall, which collects water from several sources, usually funnelling it through a downpipe to a drain.

Humification – the process of generating humus in a decomposition process, leading to a dark material with a friable texture and pleasant smell.

In-situ – processes occuring on the spot, not at a distance.

Inspection chamber – covered subsurface chamber giving access to sewerage pipework for inspection and maintenance.

Leachates – excess liquors generated during decomposition of organic materials which slowly trickle out from a compost mass.

Leachfield – subsurface gravel-filled trenches dug into soil (of suitable porosity) to which wastewater is discharged for treatment by filtration and digestion by soil bacteria.

Mouldering – a relatively slow decomposition process often involving fungi and invertebrate decomposers.

Nutrients – any of a number of chemical compounds needed by plants for nutrition and growth, the principal among these being compounds of nitrogen, phosphorus and potassium.

Organic wastes – wastes of biological origin; for the household the principal sources are domestic food wastes, garden wastes, toilet wastes.

Pathogenic wastes – wastes which could potentially cause diseases owing to the presence of disease- causing organisms or pathogens; basically anything contaminated with *faeces*.

Pathogens – organisms deleterious to human health.

Porcelain Standard – the norm of perceived hygiene and gentility set by the conventional WC in a conventional setting.

Privy – a traditional dry toilet, usually situated in an outhouse.

Putrescibles – moist, readily decomposable organic material such as vegetable matter or food waste.

Rodding eye – small aperture on the lid of a septic tank through which a rod can be inserted to clear blockages from T-shaped pipework (q.v. dip pipe).

RPMS – recycled papermill sludge or de-inking sludge. This is a material left over from paper recycling with a high content of clay, cellulose fibres and calcium, but with low toxicity.

Septic Tank – chamber or series of chambers designed to hold liquid wastes in order to settle out or liquefy some of the solid matter, providing an effluent that is safely releasable into the soil. Simple, no moving parts: the commonest alternative to sewage connection. Proven technology, but performance does not always satisfy modern standards.

Septic tank effluent – partially treated wastewater flowing out of a septic tank for further treatment elsewhere.

Sewage – toilet and liquid biological wastes; essentially *faeces*, urine + *greywater*; in this booklet usually meaning toilet wastes.

Sewer – an underground pipe or channel which collects waste water for further treatment or disposal. **Sewerage:** a system of sewers carrying liquid waste to treatment or discharge points.

Sewage sludge – in the context of septic tanks, any semi-solid matter which needs to be removed from time to time.

Shock load – effluent inputs to a sewage treatment system of grey- or blackwater (q.v.) in excess of those normally to be expected for that situation.

Soak – dry material added to the sewage mass in many *dry toilets* to inhibit smells, absorb excess liquid, adjust the *carbon-to nitrogen ratio* and maintain an open structure to foster *aerobic conditions*.

Soakaway – a hole in the ground into which waste waters can drain away; it is usually filled with loose rocks or coarse gravel.

Soil pipe – pipe carrying sewage and wastewater from the toilet pedestal to a place of treatment or sewer.

Straw Trap – a free-draining container packed with straw to catch solid particles from a waste water stream.

Take Up – the extent to which a system or principle is adopted in society as a whole.

Thermophilic – an aerobic decomposition process that generates high temperatures (above 50 degrees C). It is likely to kill pathogens in the compost mass.

Toilet Pedestal – the part of a toilet system which projects above ground level, and on which western users sit. Males customarily urinate standing into the pedestal.

Toilet System – a system which collects, transports and processes human wastes.

Trench Arch – an experimental treatment system in which waste water is run onto gravel or bare soil in a long trench, covered with a rigid structure of some kind, often with an arch-like cross-section

Twin-vault toilet – a *composting toilet* in which two chambers or 'vaults' alternate, one active, the other sealed while completing its composting process. The objective is to avoid handling uncomposted sewage and not to rely for success on efficient aerobic conditions.

Undercroft – space under a building in which installations such as a composting chamber might be sited.

Urinal – a device designed to collect urine, usually from male users. The urine is piped away for further treatment.

Index

New Futures

Sustainable environmental solutions from C.A.T. Publications.

The following books in this series are now available.

For a full publications list including Resource Guides applicable to this book, send an A5 SAE to C.A.T.

General Technology

Off the Grid: Managing Independent Renewable Electricity Systems
Allen, P. and Todd, R. (1995), NF6, 60pp, £5.50
Power Plants: A Guide to Biofuels
Horne, B. (1996), NF16, 64pp, £5.50

Windpower

It's a Breeze — A Guide to Choosing Windpower
Piggott, H. (1995), NF13, 36pp, £4.50
Windpower Workshop
Piggott, H. (1997), NF14, 160pp, £10.00

Solar Power

Tapping the Sun: A Solar Water Heating Guide
Horne, B. (1994), NF1, 16pp, £3.50
Solar Water Heating: A DIY Guide
Trimby, P. (1994), NF10, 32pp, £4.95

Energy Conservation

**Save Energy Save Money:
A Guide to Energy Conservation in the Home**
Jackson, F. (1995), NF2, 40pp, £5.30

Environmental Building

The Whole House Book: Ecological Building Design and Materials
Borer, P. and Harris, C. (1998), NF19, 320pp, £29.95
Out of the Woods: Ecological Designs for Timber Frame Self Build
Borer, P. and Harris, C. (1994), NF11, 124pp, £13.95

The Water Cycle

Safe to Drink? The Quality of Your Water
Stauffer, J. (1996), NF8, 160pp, £7.95
Sewage Solutions: Answering the Call of Nature
Grant, N., Moodie, M. and Weedon, C. (1996), NF12, 160pp, £10.00
Fertile Waste: Managing Your Domestic Sewage
Harper, P. (1994), NF3, 32pp, £3.95